Essentials of Financial Management

Jason Laws

T0339187

LIVERPOOL UNIVERSITY PRESS

First published as an ebook 2018 by

Liverpool University Press
4 Cambridge Street
Liverpool L69 7ZU

This paperback version first published 2019

British Library Cataloguing-in-Publication data

A British Library CIP record is available

Cover image: Stocks and Shares (ID 84352497) © Wavebreakmedia Ltd | Dreamstime

ISBN 9781786949646 ebook
ISBN 9781786942050 paperback

Typeset by Carnegie Publishing Ltd, Lancaster
Printed by BooksFactory.co.uk

Contents

Introduction

This book is aimed at students who have only an elementary knowledge of financial concepts. It considers the following big decisions that all companies have to address:

1. how to raise capital
2. how to decide in which projects to invest the capital
3. how to determine the distribution of excess cash flows
4. how to manage risk

This book deals with all of these questions.

My philosophy regarding the teaching of finance is that it is a real-life subject and an applied discipline. The approach in this book follows this philosophy. Where applicable, real-world examples are provided and, where appropriate, examples are supported by spreadsheet solutions. To help with your understanding, please view the Excel solution for each exercise and example, and determine for yourself how the answer changes when key input data is varied.

The content of this book is drawn from materials developed and delivered at Liverpool John Moores University and the University of Liverpool. My thanks go to the students of those universities for maintaining my love of finance. In addition I would like to thank Alison Welsby for her infinite patience and thorough editing of the manuscript. Finally, I would like to thank JISC, without whose support I would not have had the drive to complete this book.

Jason Laws, January 2018

1
An introduction to equity markets

1.1 The benefits of a smooth-running stock exchange

Why is it that stock exchanges are considered so important? Why do most national news bulletins conclude by telling their audience what the local stock exchanges have done that day?

Most developed stock exchanges around the world are considered "liquid", and shareholders are able to sell their shares quickly, at a fair price and at a low cost. In addition, shareholders know at any given point that they can sell their shares, and even if they don't wish to sell they know the value of their holdings. Because of this enhanced liquidity and transparency in pricing, shareholders are willing to supply capital to the stock market. In economics we typically solve the "scarcity" problem by allowing the market to decide what will be produced and which firms will produce it. An efficiently functioning stock market, similarly, helps allocate scarce investment capital. If the market was poorly regulated and operationally inefficient, then it is likely that we would face an inefficient allocation of capital.

In order to induce investors to provide capital to the stock market, they need to know that there is a level playing field and that the market is not skewed in the direction of investors with privileged information. If investors do not hold this view, then they will be unwilling to supply capital to the market and this will inhibit economic growth.

When a company makes the decision to go public, there is a recognition that the consequent reporting requirements are much more stringent than when it was privately owned. A privately owned company is required to publish annual reports, but when a company goes public the extent of the information that is required to be made known is increased. In the US, this is referred to as the 10K form. In addition to this, companies are required to submit a 10Q form to the Securities and Exchange Commission (SEC). There are also numerous other forms that may need to be submitted, depending on the firm's activities. Forms 3, 4 and 13D, for example, are commonly used, as they detail changes in ownership. As a result of this scrutiny, potential suppliers of capital view the firm with enhanced confidence and are more likely to invest.

While the rules and regulations vary around the world, the basic premise of an acquisition is that if one company wants to take over another company, this can be achieved by simply buying the stock in the stock market. The motives for such an acquisition are numerous but include gaining market share or technology and/or the replacement of inefficient management. Stocks that are publicly quoted are exposed to acquisitions, whereas the shares in privately owned companies are not.

1.2 The efficient market hypothesis

In section 5.2 we will cover the net present value (NPV) decision rule and in section 2.6 we will encounter the concept of beta. In an NPV decision rule, it is imperative that any real investment decisions made by a company are reflected in the company's share price. For example, if a company makes an investment with a positive NPV it should increase shareholder wealth, and the share price should rise accordingly. In determining the discount rate to evaluate projects it is imperative that the stock price and the stock market index accurately reflect relevant information.

The efficient market hypothesis was developed in 1970 by Eugene Fama, who defined three key forms of market efficiency. In the weak form, current market prices reflect all historical information about a company. In the semi-strong form, the information from the weak form is supplemented by current publicly available information about the company. Finally, the strong form requires stock prices to reflect the information included in both the weak and semi-strong forms, as well as privately held information. This is the most stringent form of market efficiency as it includes "insider" information.

One implication of a stock market having semi-strong form efficiency is that if new information relating to a company is released, the market should immediately process this information rationally, determining whether it has a positive or a negative impact on share prices and adjusting market prices accordingly. The speed of information incorporation is assumed to be so fast that there is no opportunity to buy the shares between information release and incorporation into the price. This ensures that the market is a level playing field. Information is assumed to arrive randomly and is therefore not forecastable.

Eugene Fama received the Nobel Prize for Economics in 2013. A discussion of his contribution can be found on the Nobel Prize website.[1]

1.3 Ordinary shares

Ordinary shares, often known as common stock, are the most common form of financial ownership. When a company issues ordinary shares it is never required to repay the share capital. Ordinary shares normally entitle you to vote and to receive the company's residual profit, i.e. net profit available after creditors and other providers of capital have been paid. This places ordinary shareholders in a risky situation because they stand at the back of a large queue behind the tax authorities, creditors and preference shareholders (covered later in this chapter). However, the returns to creditors such as bondholders and banks, and to preference shareholders, are fixed, whereas the returns to ordinary shareholders are potentially unlimited.

If you asked a group of students who have not previously studied finance whether a firm that has issued ordinary shares "must pay a regular dividend", the majority would say yes. However, for ordinary shares there is no guaranteed dividend, and shareholders will only receive a dividend if sufficient funds remain after other creditors have been paid and if the company chooses to pay one. The company could choose to retain the funds and use them for investment purposes.

Activity 1.1

Search online for the following term: "Alphabet certificate of incorporation". Use the resultant document to determine the difference between A shares, B shares and C shares.

Several companies have different classes of ordinary shares. One well-known company with such a structure is Berkshire Hathaway:

> Each Class A common share is entitled to one vote per share. Class B common stock possesses dividend and distribution rights equal to one-

---

[1] https://www.nobelprize.org/nobel_prizes/economic-sciences/laureates/2013/fama-facts.html

fifteen-hundredth (1/1,500) of such rights of Class A common stock. Each Class B common share possesses voting rights equivalent to one-ten-thousandth (1/10,000) of the voting rights of a Class A share.[2]

If the A shares are worth US$280,850 and the B shares are worth US$187.37, then the ratio of one to other is 1498.91, which is very close to the ratio of dividend and distribution rights (1500:1).

1.4 Preference shares

In section 1.3 we discussed ordinary shares, which are the most popular form of shares. However, another form of share capital exists in the form of preference shares. As the name suggests, preference shares are preferred to ordinary shares when it comes to the distribution of profits in the form of dividends. In addition, if a company faces financial difficulties, preference shareholders are given priority in the distribution of assets. Moreover, while the payment and size of dividends on ordinary shares are discretionary, preference shares "guarantee" a fixed dividend. However, if a firm fails to pay a preference dividend then the company will not face bankruptcy, which would be the case if a company failed to make a bond/loan payment. As the dividend is "guaranteed", from an investor's perspective it is considered a low-risk investment compared to ordinary shares, and it follows that investors will accept a lower return than from ordinary shares in the same company. In addition, preference shares usually do not have voting rights attached to them.

Examples of preference dividends

The Bank of China issued RMB 39.94 billion of preference shares in October 2014 with a nominal value per share of RMB 1,000 and a dividend rate of 6.75%.[3]

British Petroleum has two preference shares in issue. The payment details are as follows:

Payment of the dividend for the 8% and 9% cumulative preference shareholders is made on:

31 January (or the closest working day) for the half year ended 30 September; and

31 July (or the closest working day) for the half year ended 31 March.

---

[2] Berkshire Hathaway annual report (2015).
[3] http://www.boc.cn/en/investor/ir4/201501/t20150114_4462474.html

The dividend will be £0.04 (4p) per share for 8% cumulative preference shareholders and £0.045 (4.5p) per share for 9% cumulative preference shareholders.[4]

Preference shares have very similar characteristics to loan capital from the issuer's point of view, with the requirement to pay a fixed dividend each year. However, there are two distinct differences between loan capital and preference shares. Loan capital has a finite life, whereas preference shares have an infinite life. In addition, preference shareholders are considered as having ownership in the company, whereas lenders are not. As a result, interest payments can be considered as a legitimate business expense and hence deducted before taxation.

Consider two companies, A and B, which are looking to raise £100m in external financing. Company A has raised the £100m via a preference share issue with a yield of 10% p.a. Company B has issued a perpetual bond with an annual coupon payment of 10% p.a.

Is there a difference in the amount of wealth available for distribution to ordinary shareholders if they both generate profits before tax, dividends and interest of £80m?

Tax rate	26%	
Debt issue	£0.00	£100,000,000
Preference share Issue	£100,000,000	£0.00
Debt yield (%)		10%
Preference share dividend (%)	10%	

	Company A	Company B
Profits before tax, dividends and interest (1)	£80,000,000	£80,000,000
Interest payable on bonds (2)	£0.00	£10,000,000
Taxable profit (3) = (1) – (2)	£80,000,000	£70,000,000
Tax payable (4)	£20,800,000	£18,200,000
Preference dividend (5)	£10,000,000	£0.00
Available to ordinary shareholders (3) – (4) – (5)	£49,200,000	£51,800,000
Difference	£2,600,000	
Tax rate x debt issue x debt yield	£2,600,000	

---

[4] https://www.bp.com/en/global/corporate/investors/information-for-shareholders/dividends/preference-share-dividends.html

7

It is evident that the tax paid by Company A is lower than that paid by Company B, because interest paid on Company B's debt reduces the taxable profit. This results in an extra £2.6m being available for distribution to ordinary shareholders. This difference is referred to as the tax shield and can be found by: debt issue x tax rate x debt yield

The spreadsheet for this exercise can be found at https://www.liverpooluniversitypress.co.uk/pages/essentials-of-financial-management-efm. Please ensure you click on Section 1 and the 1.4 tab at the bottom of the spreadsheet.

1.5 Authorised, issued and par values

When a firm is incorporated, an amount referred to as the authorised share capital is determined. This indicates the maximum number of shares the company can issue. In the majority of cases, companies do not issue up to this amount. For example, a company may have set its authorised share capital at £200m but may only have issued £150m as shares, leaving £50m as authorised but unissued share capital. The company is then free to issue the remainder as it wishes to raise additional capital.

Ordinary shares have what is referred to as a "par value", which is usually an amount such as 100 pence or 50 pence. This bears no relation to the current market value of the shares. However, in the balance sheet of a company, the issued share capital appears as par value. The balance sheet also includes an amount referred to as the "share premium account", which reflects the difference between the amount paid for the shares at the time of issue and the par value.

Example

The equity component of the balance sheet in Speedy Hire's 2017 annual statement[5] includes the following details:

Equity	2017 (£m)	2016 (£m)
Share capital	26.2	26.1
Share premium	191.4	191.4
Merger reserve	1.0	1
Hedging reserve	(0.6)	(0.9)
Translation reserve	0.6	(1.8)
Retained earning	(29.0)	(37.5)
Total equity	**189.6**	**178.4**

Here you will notice that the share premium account remained constant at £191.4m, but the share capital account increased from £26.1m to £26.2m. The notes to the accounts state: "During the year, 0.3m ordinary shares of 5 pence were issued on exercise of options under the Speedy Hire Sharesave Schemes".[6] In addition it details that the £26.2m is made up of 523.6m ordinary shares of 5 pence each = £26,180,000

1.6 An initial public offering

An initial public offering, more commonly known as an IPO, is when a privately owned company issues stock to the wider public for the first time. By way of an example, consider the case of Facebook, which was incorporated in 2004 with equity stakes divided between the co-founders Mark Zuckerberg and Eduardo Saverin. Later in 2004, a venture capitalist, Peter Thiel, invested US$0.5m in return for a 10.2% share of the company. There then followed two further rounds of funding, referred to in the media as series A and B, when shares were sold to various venture capitalists. A third round of funding (series C) in 2007 saw 1.6% of Facebook sold to Microsoft for US$240m, implying that the value of the entire Facebook company was US$15bn. In May 2012, Facebook held an IPO when it sold an approximate 15% stake amounting to 421

[5] https://www.speedyservices.com/investors/results-reports
[6] Speedy Hire 2017 Annual Report, p. 108. The 2017 annual report can be obtained from the Speedy Hire investor relations website available at
https://www.speedyservices.com/uploads/file/3b3c1008195f47fdacf351108f221a1d/6899_Speedy_AR_2017_Web.pdf

million shares, priced at US$38 per share, giving the company an overall valuation of US$104bn and realising significant gains for the initial founders and investors.

The share performance following the IPO was initially disappointing and investors in the IPO would have suffered a loss, albeit a "paper" one. But those investors who held on to the shares for five years would have experienced gains in excess of 350%. Note, had the number of shares in issue remained static, aside from personal gains by managers and founders, Facebook, as a company, would not have benefited. However, Facebook has issued shares since the IPO at an ever higher share price, which has benefited the company tremendously.

Facebook is a classic example of a small, young company seeking both capital to expand and also a return on investment for both founders and investors. An UK example is the supermarket chain Morrisons, which started as a market stall in Bradford in 1899 and held an IPO in 1967, and now has about 500 UK supermarkets. IPOs can also be made by large privately owned companies. For example, in 1999 the previously privately owned company Goldman Sachs held an IPO, selling 12.6% of the company to the public at US$53 per share. Of the remainder, 48.3% of the company was held by 221 former partners, each holding approximately US$63m.

In an IPO the money paid by investors for the newly issued shares goes directly to the company, in what we will refer to as the primary market. Subsequent trading takes place in the secondary market, and any gains or losses are therefore independent of the issuing company and simply pass between investors.

Following an IPO, the company's founders and initial investors will see the size of their shareholdings fall as more shares are issued. However, if the capital is used wisely, the shareholders will see a rise in the absolute value of their shares. In the case of Goldman Sachs, the share price had risen to around US$230 per share at the start of 2017 from US$53 in 1999.

1.7 Stock market indices

A stock market index is a method of measuring a stock market as a whole. Stock market indices are classified in four key ways:

1. Global stock market indices gauge the performance of the world's equity markets. For example, the Financial Times All-World Index measures the performance of large and mid-cap stocks from 47 countries.

2. Regional stock market indices measure the performance of regional equity markets. For example, the Euro Stoxx 50 consists of the 50 largest, and most liquid, stocks in the Eurozone (i.e. countries having the euro as their currency).

3. National stock market indices represent the performance of the entire domestic stock market of a country. This is particularly useful since most economic indicators, such as

Gross Domestic Product, are published on a quarterly basis, whereas stock index prices are available on a second-by-second basis and therefore provide an immediate barometer of economic activity. Each country has its own important stock market index. In the UK, the leading stock market index is the FTSE100, which includes the 100 largest UK companies. In addition, it represents approximately 80% of the capitalisation of the entire UK stock market.

4. Focused indices track specific sectors of the economy or specific types of shares. For example, the S&P Global Luxury index represents the performance of 80 stocks engaged in "luxury" activities. Notable inclusions are LVMH-Moet Vuitton, Tesla and Daimler.

Activity 1.2

Search online for the following term: "FTSE250 chart". Note the value of the index on 23 June 2016 and 24 June 2016.

1.8 Stock market linkages

As noted above, a stock market index can be considered a barometer of economic activity. In addition, as world economies are exposed to many of the same systematic issues, they have a tendency to move together. Consider the following scatter diagram:

Scatter diagram of FTSE100 against S&P500 (weekly changes, 2012-2017

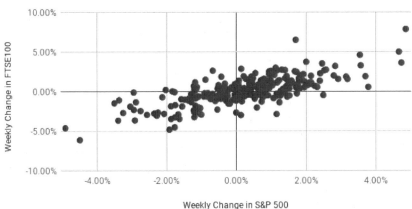

Weekly Change in S&P 500

It is evident that the two stock market indices have a tendency to move together. In fact, over the 261 weeks analysed, the two series moved in the same direction for 196 weeks (75%) and in the opposite direction for 65 weeks (25%). A more formal way of communicating this information is to say that the correlation between the weekly returns is 0.73 and is therefore positive. Correlation takes on the following values:

Correlation = –1: two series are said to be perfectly negatively correlated.

Correlation = +1: two series are said to be perfectly positively correlated.

Correlation = 0: two series exhibit no discernible relationship.

We could say therefore that FTSE100 and S&P500 weekly returns are strongly positively correlated.

The spreadsheet for this exercise can be found at https://www.liverpooluniversitypress.co.uk/pages/essentials-of-financial-management-efm. Please ensure you click on Section 1 and the 1.8a tab at the bottom of the spreadsheet.

Consider the following correlation matrix, calculated using five years of weekly returns data for a range of stock market indices.

	FTSE100	S&PCOMP	CHSASHR	ASX200I	DAXINDX	JSEOVER
FTSE100	1	0.73	0.18	0.62	0.76	0.69
S&PCOMP	0.73	1	0.17	0.52	0.71	0.58
CHSASHR	0.18	0.17	1	0.12	0.15	0.23
ASX200I	0.62	0.52	0.12	1	0.54	0.57
DAXINDX	0.76	0.71	0.15	0.54	1	0.63
JSEOVER	0.69	0.58	0.23	0.57	0.63	1

FTSE100 – FTSE 100 index (UK); S&PCOMP – Standard and Poors 500 Index (US); CHSASHR – Shanghai A share index (China); ASX200I – Australian Stock Exchange Index; DAXINDX – DAX 30 Index (Germany); JSEOVER – Johannesburg Stock Index (South Africa).

The most strongly correlated indices over this period are the DAX in Germany and the FTSE100 in the UK. The most weakly correlated indices over this period are the Shanghai A share index and the Australian Stock Exchange index. Note that all of the calculated correlations are positive.

The spreadsheet for this exercise can be found at https://www.liverpooluniversitypress.co.uk/pages/essentials-of-financial-management-efm. Please ensure you click on Section 1 and the 1.8b tab at the bottom of the spreadsheet.

1.9 Rights issues

Once a company has a listing on the stock exchange it can raise additional capital via a rights issue. In a rights issue, existing shareholders are offered the opportunity to buy additional shares at a price that is usually a discount from the prevailing market price. There is no requirement for existing shareholders to accept the offer and they are permitted to sell the rights on. A rights issue usually takes place on a ratio basis. For example, in 2015 Tata Motors raised new capital via a rights issue that offered six new shares for every 109 shares held. This would be a 6-for-109 rights issue.

If you buy shares in a company that is undertaking a rights issue then two important terms are used: cum-rights and ex-rights. Shares that are labelled as cum-rights provide the opportunity to take part in the rights issue, whereas shares that are labelled ex-rights do not. In the latter case, the opportunity to take part in the rights issue resides with the previous shareholder.

Example

Consider a company, Riverbank plc, that wishes to raise capital for investment yet is reluctant to borrow the money in the capital markets. Instead it seeks to raise money via a rights issue. In order to attract investors, it will need to offer existing shareholders the opportunity to buy new shares below the current market price. This is not only attractive to investors but avoids the risk of the share price falling between the beginning and the completion of the rights issue.

Riverbank has decided it will raise £50m by issuing 25m shares at a price of 225p each. As Riverbank plc presently has 100m shares in issue, the rights issue will be a 1-for-4 rights issue, i.e. the ratio of 25m new shares to 100m old shares. The pre-rights issue share price is 250p.

Clearly the share price cannot remain at 250p following the rights issue. In order to determine the ex-rights share price, we can consider the total capitalisation of the company:

> Total capitalisation pre rights issue = £250m
>
> Capital raised = £56.25m
>
> Total market capitalisation = £306.25m
>
> Total shares available = 125m
>
> Ex-rights share price = 245p

Alternatively, you can examine the situation from the viewpoint of an investor holding four existing shares who participates in the rights issue:

> Four existing shares at a price of 250p = 1000p
>
> One new share for cash at 225p = 225p
>
> Total value of five shares = 1225p
>
> Value of one share (ex-rights) = 245p

A common misconception is that, because the share price has fallen, the investor must lose out. Our investor holding four shares, who took up the rights issue, has lost 5 pence for each share, a loss of 20p in total. However, they purchased one new share for 225p via the rights issue, which is now worth 245p. Therefore, the shareholder experiences a decline in the price of the old shares, but this loss is exactly offset by the gain in share value on the new rights issue shares. The gain/loss can also be considered as the value of a right on one share, which in this example is:

$$\frac{Market\ value\ of\ shares\ \text{ex-rights} - subscription\ price}{Number\ of\ shares\ required\ to\ purchase\ one\ new\ share}$$

plugging in the data:

$$\frac{245 - 225}{4} = 5p$$

Hence the value of a right for someone holding four shares is 20p.

1.10 Stock splits

The nominal book value of a company's shares is defined as:

number of shares in issue x nominal value of each share

In a stock split, the nominal value of each share is reduced while at the same time there is a proportional increase in the number of outstanding shares. The net effect is that the nominal book value remains unchanged. For example, a company may have 10m shares in issue with a nominal value of 50p each (nominal book value = 10m x 50p = £5m). In order to achieve a stock split, the firm issues a further 10m shares to existing shareholders with the nominal value of each share reducing to 25p each. The nominal book value is now 20m x 25p = £5m. The motivation for doing this is often counter-intuitive to students, as clearly the share price will fall. However, as the post-stock-split share price is reduced, the stock becomes more attractive to investors. In fact, in 2014, Google (now Alphabet) undertook a 2-for-1 stock split following the rise in the share price to above US$1,000 per share. This higher share price was considered unattractive to individual investors.

Apple has held numerous stock splits since 1987 as detailed below:[7]

Date	Stock split
June 2014	7-for-1 stock split
February 2005	2-for-1 stock split
June 2000	2-for-1 stock split
June 1987	2-for-1 stock split

In June 1987, 1 original share became 2 shares, which in June 2000 became 4 shares, which in February 2005 became 8 shares; finally, in June 2014, these 8 shares became 56 shares. Therefore if, in 2017, the Apple share price is around US$150 per share, this actually represents 56 x US$150 of the original share's US$8,400. The original IPO price in 1980 was around US$22!

---

[7] http://investor.apple.com/dividends.cfm

Activity 1.3

Search online for the following terms: "Microsoft stock split history" and "Microsoft stock price". Obtain the current market price for Microsoft and compare this to the original IPO price of around US$21.

A reverse stock split is less common but not unknown when the company wishes to increase the share price. In a reverse stock split, the number of outstanding shares is reduced and the share price increases proportionately. For example, if you own 10,000 shares in a company and it declares a 1-for-10 reverse split, you will own a total of 1,000 shares after the split, albeit at a higher price. Therefore, a reverse stock split has no effect on the overall value of what shareholders own. In May 2011, Citigroup held a 1-for-10 reverse split.[8] The impact of the stock split is shown in the table below:

Date	Open	High	Low	Close	Volume
05/05/2011	4.49	4.51	4.46	4.48	27190000
06/05/2011	4.55	4.58	4.5	4.52	5131700
09/05/2011	44.89	45.12	43.85	44.16	49168100
10/05/2011	44.01	44.53	43.75	44.2	42299000

You can see that the reverse stock split had the desired effect in boosting the lowly share price from around US$4.5 to over US$44.

1.11 Share repurchase

A share repurchase (or buy-back) is similar to a dividend in that a company is distributing wealth to shareholders. Under a share buy-back a company repurchases its shares at the prevailing market value (or at a premium), thereby reducing the number of shares outstanding. The rationale for this is that the management may feel that the stock price is too low and that buying its own shares may give a positive signal to the market. Alternatively, it may be viewed as a way of returning wealth to shareholders. For example, during 2010, 2011 and 2012, Astra Zeneca repurchased shares amounting to US$2,604m, US$6,015m and US$2,635 respectively. One of the best-known long-term share repurchase schemes is that of Home Depot, which,

---

[8] http://www.citigroup.com/citi/investor/ajax/split.html

since 2002, has repurchased stock having a value of approximately US$67.1 billion, as it returns wealth to shareholders. We will see in later sections that the value of an asset or a company is found by discounting future cash flows at a discount rate that represents the risk of future operations. A share repurchase does not change the risk of the future cash flows, but it does change two notable financial ratios: return on assets and earnings per share.

The example below demonstrates this case.

Example

Suppose a company repurchases two million shares at £5 per share for a total cash outlay of £10m.

If before the repurchase it had £40m cash, total assets of £70m, earnings of £5m and 20m outstanding shares, what would be the impact of the repurchase on the return on assets (ROA) and earnings per share (EPS)?

	Before repurchase	**Post-repurchase**
Cash (1)	£40,000,000	£30,000,000
Assets (2)	£70,000,000	£60,000,000
Earnings (3)	£5,000,000	£5,000,000
Shares outstanding (4)	20m	18m
Return on assets (5) = (3)/(2)	7.14%	8.33%
Earnings per share = (3)/(4)	0.25	0.28

The company's cash has been reduced from £40m to £30m, which in turn lowers the total assets of the company from £70m to £60m. This then leads to an increase in its ROA, even though earnings have not changed. A similar effect can be seen in the EPS number, which increases from 0.25 to 0.28. The buy-back also helps to improve the company's price–earnings ratio (P/E), since if we assume that the shares remain at £5, the P/E ratio before the buy-back is 20 (£5/0.25). After the buy-back, the P/E decreases to 18 (£5/£0.28) due to the reduction in outstanding shares. From an investor's perspective, a lower P/E ratio is preferable as you are paying less of a multiple of a company's earnings.

The spreadsheet for this exercise can be found at https://www.liverpooluniversitypress. co.uk/pages/essentials-of-financial-management-efm. Please ensure you click on Section 1 and the 1.11 tab at the bottom of the spreadsheet.

2
Risk versus return

2.1 A primer on the variance of an asset and covariance of a pair of assets

One of the basic pillars of finance is "the greater the risk, the greater the return". In finance, risk is measured by dispersion from the mean. Consider the following two assets, both of which have an average return of 10% over the past twelve months.

Month	Stock A	Stock B
1	5	0
2	15	20
3	10	10
4	5	0
5	15	20
6	10	10
7	5	0
8	15	20
9	10	10
10	5	0
11	15	20
12	10	10
Average	**10**	**10**

If we analyse the data it appears evident that stock B's returns are more erratic than stock A's. In order to quantify this variability we need to find the variance of each stock's returns. This is found using a population variance:

$$\sigma_i^2 = \frac{1}{n} \sum_{i=1}^{n} (R_i - \bar{R}_i)^2$$

Applying this to stock prices, we need to find the deviation of each period's return (R_i) from the average return over the period ($\bar{R}_i$).

Stock A – ave(A)	Stock B – ave(B)
−5	−10
5	10
0	0
−5	−10
5	10
0	0
−5	−10
5	10
0	0
−5	−10
5	10
0	0

It is clear that the stock which we view to be more erratic has greater deviations from the mean. The next step is to square these deviations from the mean and sum them together as follows:

[Stock A – ave(A)]²	[Stock B – ave(B)]²
25	100
25	100
0	0
25	100
25	100
0	0
25	100
25	100

	[Stock A – ave(A)]²	[Stock B – ave(B)]²
	0	0
	25	100
	25	100
	0	0
Sum	**200**	**800**

It is evident from the table above that larger deviations from the mean contribute to a greater sum total. If we divided these figures of 200 and 800 respectively by N, which in this case is 12, we arrive at the variance of each asset:

variance of asset A = 200/12 = 16.67

variance of asset B = 800/12 = 66.67

The units of variance are rather unusual, as for stock return data they would be considered as percentages squared. If we take the square root of the variance, we obtain the standard deviation, which is expressed in percentages, making it a more attractive measure, since percentages are a familiar metric in finance, being used in interest rates, growth rates, inflation etc.

standard deviation of asset A = $\sqrt{16.67}$ = 4.08%

standard deviation of asset B = $\sqrt{66.67}$ = 8.16%

The interpretation of the standard deviation of stock returns is: the higher the number, the more variable the return and the greater the risk. At the absolute limit, if a stock did not deviate from its average return, the standard deviation would be zero.

Applying the above approach to twelve months' stock data for MGM we find the following:

Date	MGM	MGM	MGM-average	(MGM-average)²
01/11/2016	28.71			
01/12/2016	28.83	0.42%	−0.0042	0.0000
01/01/2017	28.8	−0.10%	−0.0095	0.0001
01/02/2017	26.29	−8.72%	−0.0956	0.0091
01/03/2017	27.4	4.22%	0.0338	0.0011
01/04/2017	30.71	12.08%	0.1124	0.0126
01/05/2017	31.72	3.29%	0.0245	0.0006
01/06/2017	31.29	−1.36%	−0.0220	0.0005
01/07/2017	32.93	5.24%	0.0440	0.0019
01/08/2017	32.96	0.09%	−0.0075	0.0001

Date	MGM	MGM	MGM-average	(MGM-average)^2
01/09/2017	32.59	−1.12%	−0.0196	0.0004
01/10/2017	31.03	−4.79%	−0.0563	0.0032
	Average	**0.84%**	**Sum**	**0.0296**
			Variance = sum/N	**0.0027**
			Standard deviation = sqrt	**5.19%**

This is a monthly standard deviation. In order to convert this to an annualised value, we would multiply by the square root of 12 to get 17.98%.

Obtaining the covariance is similar:

$$\sigma_{ij} = \frac{1}{n}\sum_{i=1}^{n}(R_i - \bar{R}_i)(R_j - \bar{R}_j)$$

However, here, rather than squaring the deviations from the mean, we multiply the deviation from the mean, for stock i, by the deviation from the mean, for stock j. Returning to our stocks A and B from earlier:

Month	Stock A	Stock B	Stock A − ave(A)	Stock B − ave(B)	[Stock A − ave(A)] *[Stock B − ave(B)]
1	5	0	−5	−10	50
2	15	20	5	10	50
3	10	10	0	0	0
4	5	0	−5	−10	50
5	15	20	5	10	50
6	10	10	0	0	0
7	5	0	−5	−10	50
8	15	20	5	10	50
9	10	10	0	0	0
10	5	0	−5	−10	50
11	15	20	5	10	50
12	10	10	0	0	0
Average	**10**	**10**		**Sum**	**400**
s.d.	**4.08**	**8.16**		**Covariance**	**33.33**

Stocks A and B have a tendency to move in the same direction as one another, the only difference being that when stock A is 5% below (above) its mean, stock B is 10% below (above) its mean. The resultant covariance is therefore positive. Unfortunately, aside from the sign (+), a covariance does not convey any further information. However, there is a relationship that links covariance and correlation together:

$$\rho_{AB} = \frac{\sigma_{AB}}{\sigma_A \sigma_B}$$

Applying this to the data above:

$$\rho_{AB} = \frac{\sigma_{AB}}{\sigma_A \sigma_B} = \frac{33.33}{4.08 \times 8.16} = 1$$

This confirms that the correlation between the returns of stocks A and B is +1, otherwise known as perfectly positively correlated.

Applying this approach to twelve months' data for MGM and Wynn Resorts, we find:

Date	MGM	Wynn	MGM	Wynn	Wynn-average	(Wynn-average)^2	(MGM-average) x (Wynn-average)
01/11/2016	28.71	101.99					
01/12/2016	28.83	91.88	0.42%	−9.91%	−0.1343	0.0180	0.0006
01/01/2017	28.8	101.43	−0.10%	10.39%	0.0688	0.0047	−0.0007
01/02/2017	26.29	96.15	−8.72%	−5.21%	−0.0872	0.0076	0.0083
01/03/2017	27.4	114.61	4.22%	19.20%	0.1568	0.0246	0.0053
01/04/2017	30.71	123.01	12.08%	7.33%	0.0381	0.0015	0.0043
01/05/2017	31.72	128.7	3.29%	4.63%	0.0111	0.0001	0.0003
01/06/2017	31.29	134.12	−1.36%	4.21%	0.0070	0.0000	−0.0002
01/07/2017	32.93	129.34	5.24%	−3.56%	−0.0708	0.0050	−0.0031
01/08/2017	32.96	138.99	0.09%	7.46%	0.0395	0.0016	−0.0003
01/09/2017	32.59	148.92	−1.12%	7.14%	0.0363	0.0013	−0.0007
01/10/2017	31.03	144.44	−4.79%	−3.01%	−0.0652	0.0043	0.0037
		Average	**0.84%**	**3.52%**	**Sum**	**0.0687**	**0.0175**
					Sum/N	**0.0062**	**0.0016**
					sqrt	**7.9%**	

Therefore, we find that stock returns of Wynn Resorts are more volatile, with a standard deviation of 7.9%. Applying the covariance formula, from above, we find the covariance to be 0.0016. As the two standard deviations are 0.0519 and 0.0790, we can then use:

$$\rho_{ij} = \frac{\sigma_{ij}}{\sigma_i \sigma_j}$$

to find the correlation:

$$\rho_{ij} = \frac{0.0016}{0.0519 \times 0.0790} = 0.39$$

As both MGM and Wynn Resorts are casino stocks, we would expect them to be positively correlated.

Activity 2.1

Calculate the correlation between United Continental Airlines and crude oil using monthly data from July 2011 to September 2017.

The spreadsheet for this exercise can be found at https://www.liverpool universitypress.co.uk/pages/essentials-of-financial-management-efm. Please ensure you click on Section 2 and the 2.1a and 2.1b tabs at the bottom of the spreadsheet.

2.2 The mean and variance of a portfolio

In this section we introduce the Markowitz approach to portfolio theory. This seminal piece of work on portfolio allocation under uncertainty was published by Harry Markowitz in the *Journal of Finance* in 1952. Activity 2.1 illustrated that two assets, the stock returns of United Continental Airlines and of crude oil, have a tendency to move in opposite directions. Hence, if we had a portfolio with some of our wealth invested in the stock of United Continental Airlines and some in crude oil, what we might experience is that on days when our airline stock fell, the price of crude oil would rise; alternatively, on days when the airline stock rose, the price of crude oil fell. The net effect is that the overall variability of our portfolio, as measured by the standard deviation, would be lower than if we simply held the airline stock or the crude oil in isolation. Hence, when computing the variance of a portfolio we also have to concern ourselves with how the asset returns vary together – the covariance. In Chapter 1, we used the term "correlation", since correlation is on a scale from –1 to +1, which makes it much easier to determine "weak" and "strong" correlation. When correlation between two assets is –1, you have the ultimate in diversification benefits, as the returns from one asset will be offset by the returns of the other, hence creating a risk-free portfolio. The graph below illustrates such an outcome. Perfect negative correlation gives a mean combined return for two securities over time equal to the mean for each of them, so the returns for the portfolio show no variability. Any returns above and below the mean for each of the assets are completely offset by the return for the other asset, so there is no variability in total returns, that is, no risk for the portfolio.

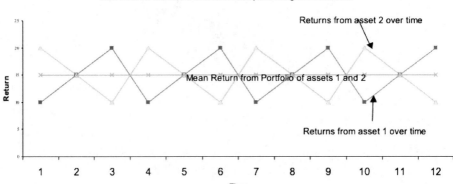

Note that correlation and covariance are linked together via the following equation:

$$\rho_{ij} = \frac{\sigma_{ij}}{\sigma_i \sigma_j}$$

where:

σ_{ij} = covariance between assets i and j

σ_i = standard deviation of asset I

σ_j = standard deviation of asset j

ρ_{ij} = correlation between assets i and j

Below we present a series of scatter diagrams between simulated returns, using three assumptions of correlation, +0.8, 0 and −0.8.

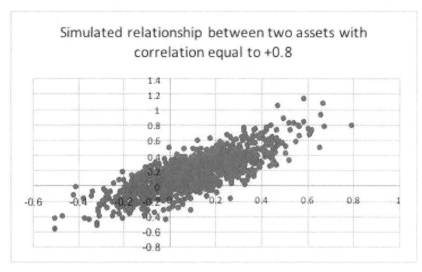

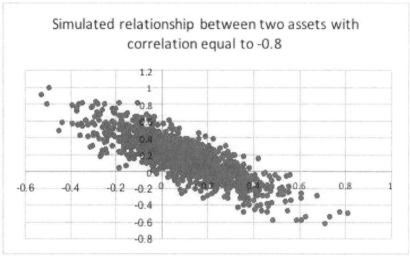

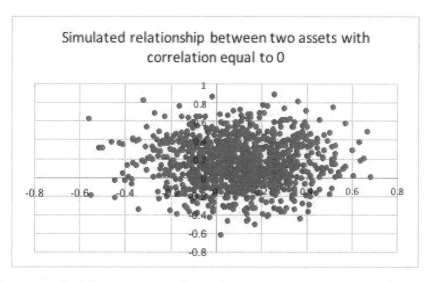

Simulated relationship between two assets with correlation equal to 0

In the analysis that follows, σ_{12} refers to the covariance between assets 1 and 2. If σ_{12} is positive, when the return on the first asset is greater than the mean value, then the return on the second asset is also, on average, greater than its mean value; and vice versa, when the return on the first asset is less than the mean value. If σ_{12} is negative, the returns on assets 1 and 2 tend to move in opposite directions and offset each other. If the return on one asset is above the mean, the return on the second will, on average, be below the mean. The fact that the returns on the assets move in opposite directions reduces the variability of the portfolio.

In general, the variance of a portfolio of assets is given by:

$$\sigma_p^2 = \sum_{i=1}^{N} X_i^2 \sigma_i^2 + \sum_{i=1}^{N} \sum_{\substack{k=1 \\ k \neq i}}^{N} X_i X_k \sigma_{ik}$$

and its standard deviation is:

$$\sigma_p = \sqrt{\sigma_p^2}$$

Consider a two-asset portfolio with proportion X_1 invested in asset 1, and X_2 $(1- X_2)$ invested in asset 2, i.e. 100% invested and no short selling. The expected return of such a portfolio is:

$$R_p = X_1 R_1 + X_2 R_2$$

The variance is then:

$$\sigma_p^2 = X_1^2 \sigma_1^2 + X_2^2 \sigma_2^2 + 2X_1 X_2 \sigma_{12}$$

Or using correlation:

$$\sigma_p^2 = X_1^2 \sigma_1^2 + X_2^2 \sigma_2^2 + 2X_1 X_2 \rho_{12} \sigma_1 \sigma_2$$

Example

Consider two stocks, Wynn Resorts and Kelloggs. The expected return (% p.a.), standard deviation (% p.a.) and correlation calculated using five years of weekly data is detailed below:

	Wynn	Kelloggs
Expected return	14.5%	5.2%
Standard deviation	36.6%	14.6%
Correlation	0.07	

Using:

$$\sigma_p^2 = X_1^2 \sigma_1^2 + X_2^2 \sigma_2^2 + 2X_1 X_2 \rho_{12} \sigma_1 \sigma_2$$

and:

$$R_p = X_1 R_1 + X_2 R_2$$

respectively to find the risk and return of portfolios with varying weights generates the following results:

W_Wynn	W_Kelloggs	Variance	s.d.	ER
0.00%	100.00%	0.0213	14.6%	5.2%
10.00%	90.00%	0.0193	13.9%	6.1%
20.00%	80.00%	0.0202	14.2%	7.1%
30.00%	70.00%	0.0241	15.5%	8.0%
40.00%	60.00%	0.0309	17.6%	8.9%
50.00%	50.00%	0.0407	20.2%	9.9%
60.00%	40.00%	0.0534	23.1%	10.8%
70.00%	30.00%	0.0691	26.3%	11.7%
80.00%	20.00%	0.0878	29.6%	12.6%

W_Wynn	W_Kelloggs	Variance	s.d.	ER
90.00%	10.00%	0.1094	33.1%	13.6%
100.00%	0.00%	0.1340	36.6%	14.5%

This can be represented graphically as:

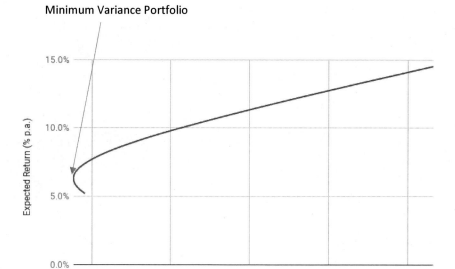

This line is referred to as the mean–standard deviation frontier. The points on the line to the right of the minimum variance portfolio are part of the efficient frontier, while points on the line to the left of the minimum variance portfolio are part of the inefficient frontier. No rational investor would select any point on the inefficient frontier, as for the same level of risk there are alternative portfolios with higher returns. Despite correlation between the two assets being positive, diversification can still reduce the risk of the portfolio.

It is evident from this graph that investors have the opportunity to reduce the risk of the portfolio, yet still increase returns, by reducing the investment in the low-risk asset (Kelloggs) and increasing the investment in the higher-risk asset (Wynn Resorts). There is one combination between the two assets whereby the risk of the portfolio, standard deviation, is minimised. In order to find this weight we need to use a little calculus:

$$\sigma_p^2 = X_1^2\sigma_1^2 + X_2^2\sigma_2^2 + 2X_1X_2\rho_{12}\sigma_1\sigma_2$$

If we are fully invested then:

$$X_1 + X_2 = 1$$

and:

$$X_2 = 1 - X_1$$

Therefore:

$$\sigma_p^2 = X_1^2\sigma_1^2 + (1 - X_1)^2\sigma_2^2 + 2X_1(1 - X_1)\rho_{12}\sigma_1\sigma_2$$

Multiplying out the brackets:

$$\sigma_p^2 = X_1^2\sigma_1^2 + \sigma_2^2 - 2X_1\sigma_2^2 + X_1^2\sigma_2^2 + 2X_1\rho_{12}\sigma_1\sigma_2 - 2X_1^2\rho_{12}\sigma_1\sigma_2$$

We should now differentiate σ_p^2 with respect to X_1:

$$\frac{\delta\sigma_p^2}{\delta X_1} = 2X_1\sigma_1^2 - 2\sigma_2^2 + 2X_1\sigma_2^2 + 2\rho_{12}\sigma_1\sigma_2 - 4X_1\rho_{12}\sigma_1\sigma_2$$

Setting this equal to zero and dividing through by 2.

$$\frac{\delta\sigma_p^2}{\delta X_1} = 0 \longrightarrow X_1\sigma_1^2 + X_1\sigma_2^2 - 2X_1\rho_{12}\sigma_1\sigma_2 = \sigma_2^2 - \rho_{12}\sigma_1\sigma_2$$

$$X_1(\sigma_1^2 + \sigma_2^2 - 2\rho_{12}\sigma_1\sigma_2) = \sigma_2^2 - \rho_{12}\sigma_1\sigma_2$$

Hence:

$$X_1 = \frac{\sigma_2^2 - \rho_{12}\sigma_1\sigma_2}{(\sigma_1^2 + \sigma_2^2 - 2\rho_{12}\sigma_1\sigma_2)}$$

and $X_2 = 1 - X_1$:

$$X_2 = \frac{\sigma_1^2 - \rho_{12}\sigma_1\sigma_2}{(\sigma_1^2 + \sigma_2^2 - 2\rho_{12}\sigma_1\sigma_2)}$$

Applying this to our Wynn and Kelloggs example

$$X_1 = \frac{\sigma_2^2 - \rho_{12}\sigma_1\sigma_2}{\sigma_1^2 + \sigma_2^2 - 2\rho_{12}\sigma_1\sigma_2} = \frac{0.366^2 - 0.07 \times .366 \times .146}{0.366^2 + 0.146^2 - 0.07 \times .366 \times .146} = 11.89\%$$

$X_2 = 88.11\%$

The risk of this portfolio is then 13.9%.

A special case exists when correlation equals –1:

$$X_1 = \frac{\sigma_2^2 - \rho_{12}\sigma_1\sigma_2}{\sigma_1^2 + \sigma_2^2 - 2\rho_{12}\sigma_1\sigma_2} = \frac{\sigma_2^2 + \sigma_1\sigma_2}{\sigma_1^2 + \sigma_2^2 + 2\rho_{12}\sigma_1\sigma_2} = \frac{\sigma_2(\sigma_1 + \sigma_2)}{(\sigma_1 + \sigma_2)^2} = \frac{\sigma_2}{(\sigma_1 + \sigma_2)}$$

In the previous diagram the correlation between the two assets was close to zero, at 0.07. This determined the shape of the mean–standard deviation frontier. The diagrams below illustrate what happens to the shape of the mean–standard deviation frontier when correlation takes the following values: (i) 1, (ii) 0.25, (iii) 0, (iv) –0.5, (v), –1.

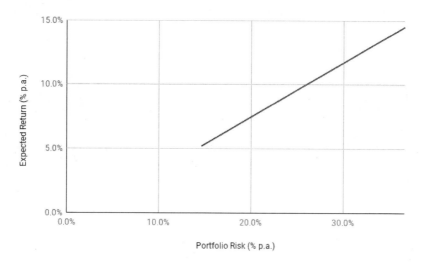

Correlation = +1

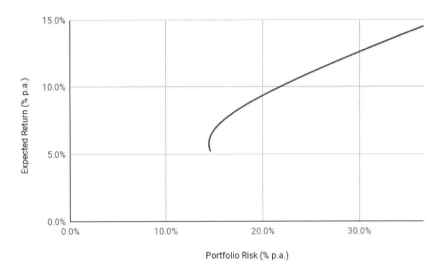

Correlation = 0.25

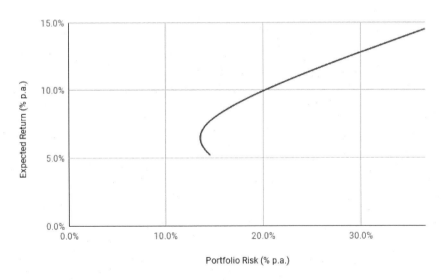

Correlation = 0

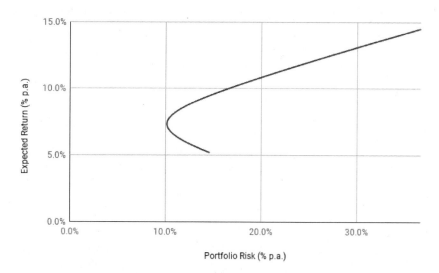

Correlation = –0.5

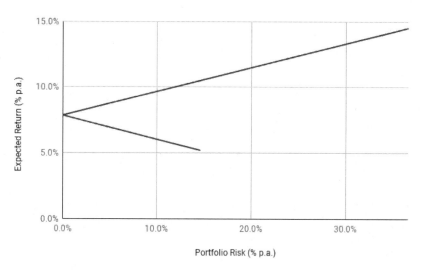

Correlation = –1

As correlation reduces, the mean–standard deviation frontier becomes more convex and the minimum variance portfolio gets closer and closer to the horizontal axis.

The spreadsheet for this exercise can be found at https://www.liverpooluniversitypress.co.uk/pages/essentials-of-financial-management-efm. Please ensure you click on Section 2 and the 2.2 tab at the bottom of the spreadsheet.

The diagram above shows that there exists one portfolio with zero risk.

This can be found using:

$$X_1 = \frac{\sigma_2}{(\sigma_1 + \sigma_2)} = \frac{14.60}{36.60 + 14.60} = 28.52\%$$

2.3 Finding the risk of a three- or more asset portfolio

Earlier we noted that the number of covariance terms (and hence correlations) required to find the risk of a N asset portfolio is N(N – 1)/2. In addition to this we require the individual variances. Therefore, to find the risk of a four-asset portfolio, the appropriate equation would be:

$$\sigma_p^2 = X_1^2\sigma_1^2 + X_2^2\sigma_2^2 + +X_3^2\sigma_3^2 + X_4^2\sigma_4^2 + 2X_1X_2\sigma_{12} + 2X_1X_3\sigma_{13} \\ + 2X_1X_4\sigma_{14} + 2X_2X_3\sigma_{23} + 2X_2X_4\sigma_{24} + 2X_3X_4\sigma_{34}$$

Note the inclusion of six covariance terms i.e. (4 x 3)/2 = 6).

This can be written in matrix notation as:

$$\sigma_p^2 = X'\Sigma X$$

where X is a (N x 1) column vector of portfolio weights, Σ is a (N x N) covariance matrix and X' is the transpose of X and has the dimensions 1 x N. If we multiply X'Σ we multiply a (1 x N) vector by a N x N matrix and the result will be a 1 x N vector. We can then multiply this result by the N x 1 vector, X, and the result will be 1 x 1, i.e. a single number and this will represent the variance.

Excel has two useful functions for matrix operations, MMULT and TRANSPOSE, which make matrix operations extremely easy.

Applying this approach to a four-asset portfolio comprising United Continental Airlines and Exxon Mobil together with Wynn Resorts and Kelloggs from earlier, we find the following results using inputs calculated using five years of weekly data:

Covariance matrix		UAL	Exxon	Wynn	Kelloggs	
Sigma	**UAL**	0.00266330	0.00014188	0.00048791	0.00015992	
	Exxon	0.00014188	0.00045895	0.00024267	0.00011834	
	WYNN	0.00048791	0.00024267	0.00257027	0.00007148	
	K	0.00015992	0.00011834	0.00007148	0.00041109	

	UAL	Exxon	Wynn	Kelloggs		
Average return	0.46%	0.01%	0.28%	0.10%		
s.d.	5.16%	2.14%	5.07%	2.03%		
s.d. (per annum)	37.2%	15.4%	36.6%	14.6%		

X	0.25	X'	0.25	0.25	0.25	0.25
	0.25					
	0.25					
	0.25					
X'S	0.0008633	0.0002405	0.0008431	0.0001902		

X'SX	0.000534	

s.d.	**2.31%**	
s.d. (per annum)	**16.67%**	

This approach is scalable, and using matrix notation it is a trivial exercise to find the risk of large asset portfolios.

The spreadsheet for this exercise can be found at https://www.liverpooluniversitypress.co.uk/pages/essentials-of-financial-management-efm. Please ensure you click on Section 2 and the 2.3 tab at the bottom of the spreadsheet.

2.4 Choosing the optimal portfolio

Each of us has different preferences regarding the decisions we make in life. This includes the selection of risk and return combinations from a large pool of choices. The previous section introduced the mean–standard deviation function, and while it is evident that no rational individual would choose a point on the inefficient frontier, how do we determine what point an individual investor will choose on the efficient frontier? The answer is found by finding the tangency point between the efficient frontier and an investor's indifference curve. The shape of an investor's indifference curve will depend on how much compensation they require in return for bearing risk. An investor with a very steep indifference curve requires a large increase in return for small increases in risk, whereas an investor with very flat indifference curve requires a small increase in return for small increases in risk.

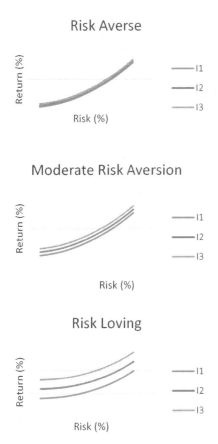

The diagram below shows the portfolio selected by a risk-averse investor (investor A) who has steep preferences and a risk-seeking investor (investor B) who has flatter preferences. In order to determine which portfolio is optimal for a given investor, we need to find the point of tangency between the mean–standard deviation frontier and the investor's indifference curve.

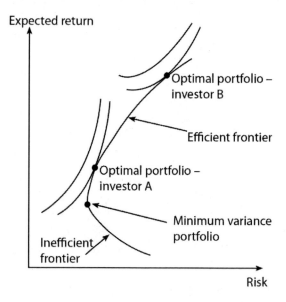

In the diagram above, investor A's optimal portfolio is on the efficient frontier, a little way along from the minimum variance portfolio. Investor B, who has flatter preferences, would select a portfolio further along the efficient frontier and select a portfolio with higher risk and higher return. As indifference curves for all investors are upward sloping, it is impossible to find a tangency point on the inefficient part of the mean–standard deviation frontier. In order for an investor to select the minimum variance portfolio, their indifference curves would need to be extremely steep to achieve the tangency condition at that point.

2.5 The risk of large portfolios

What happens to the variance of a portfolio as the number of assets increases? Recall again the formula for calculating the variance of a portfolio:

$$\sigma_p^2 = \sum_{i=1}^{N} X_i^2 \sigma_i^2 + \sum_{i=1}^{N} \sum_{\substack{k=1 \\ k \neq i}}^{N} X_i X_k \sigma_{ik}$$

Note there are N(N –1) elements inside the double summation signs since each of the N assets can be combined with any of the remaining N –1 assets. Assume further that all assets are held in equal proportions such that $X_i = X_k = 1/N$.

$$\sigma_p^2 = \sum_{i=1}^{N} \left(\frac{1}{N}\right)^2 \sigma_i^2 + \sum_{i=1}^{N}\sum_{\substack{k=1 \\ k \neq i}}^{N} \left(\frac{1}{N}\right)\left(\frac{1}{N}\right) \sigma_{ik}$$

$$\sigma_p^2 = \frac{1}{N}\frac{1}{N} \sum_{i=1}^{N} \sigma_i^2 + \frac{1}{N}\frac{1}{N} \sum_{i=1}^{N}\sum_{\substack{k=1 \\ k \neq i}}^{N} \sigma_{ik}$$

$$\sigma_p^2 = \frac{1}{N}\frac{1}{N} \sum_{i=1}^{N} \sigma_i^2 + \frac{1}{N}\frac{1}{N} \left(\frac{N-1}{N-1}\right) \sum_{i=1}^{N}\sum_{\substack{k=1 \\ k \neq i}}^{N} \sigma_{ik}$$

Note that the inclusion of the term (N –1)/(N –1) (i.e. 1) is simply to help us find the final result later.

We could write expressions for the average covariance and variances as:

$$\overline{\sigma_p^2} = \frac{1}{N} \sum_{i=1}^{N} \sigma_i^2$$

and

$$\overline{\sigma_{ik}} = \frac{1}{N(N-1)} \sum_{i=1}^{N}\sum_{\substack{k=1 \\ k \neq i}}^{N} \sigma_{ik}$$

Thus we can replace the first term with (1/N) multiplied by the average variance, and the second term with (N –1)/N multiplied by the average covariance:

$$\sigma_p^2 = \frac{1}{N}\overline{\sigma_p^2} + \frac{N-1}{N}\overline{\sigma_{ik}}$$

It is evident that as N gets large, 1/N tends towards zero, hence the first term will become less significant. With regard to the second term, as N gets large, (N –1)/N tends towards 1. Therefore, for large, equally weighted portfolios, the portfolio risk is equal to the average covariance. An important conclusion from this is that individual risks of securities can be diversified away but contribution to total risk from the covariance cannot.

Graphically, this outcome can be represented as follows:

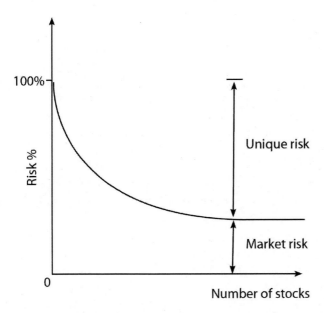

A common misconception is that if an investor adds more and more stocks to a portfolio, the portfolio risk will eventually become zero. The diagram above shows that this is not the case, since the portfolio risk tends towards the average covariance, which we refer to as "market risk". Note further that adding stocks to a portfolio will incur transaction costs, and as we add more and more stocks to the portfolio ultimately the benefits from diversification (i.e. risk reduction) will be offset by the costs of diversification (i.e. transaction costs). It is often argued that risk reduction can best be achieved using 25–30 stocks.

2.6 Market risk

As noted in section 1.6, a stock market can be considered as a barometer of economic activity. Moreover, a company's stock price reflects the value of its assets plus the present value of future opportunities. It follows that the majority of companies will benefit in an economy that is doing well but will be disadvantaged in a struggling economy. This explains why stocks have a tendency to move together and, regardless of the number of stocks an investor holds, investors are exposed to changes in the stock market. This is referred to as market risk and cannot be diversified away.

The risk that can be diversified away is called "unique risk". A unique risk is one that is particular to just that stock. For example, in April 2010, an explosion on board the drilling rig *Deepwater Horizon* caused the share price of BP to fall from approximately 650 pence to 300 pence by the end of June. This risk was unique to BP and independent of how the market moved over this period.

Following the mass shooting in Las Vegas in October 2017, casino stocks such as MGM Resorts (which owns the Mandalay Bay Hotel from where the gunman opened fire), Melco Resorts and Entertainment, Wynn Resorts and Las Vegas Sands Corp all fell. Over the period 29 September 2017 to 20 October 2017 all four casino stocks have fallen:

MGM: –4.8%, LVS: –2.3%, Wynn: –3.0%, MLCO: –0.9%.

Meanwhile, the S&P500 index has risen 2.2%. Therefore an investor with a diversified portfolio would not have been impacted by these falls, as they would have been mitigated by rises elsewhere in the portfolio.

In section 2.4 it was demonstrated that for large portfolios we require N x (N –1) different covariance terms. Thus, to undertake this type of portfolio analysis on a 100-asset portfolio we would require 9,900 different covariance terms (although covariance is symmetric, so we would actually "only" need 4,450). If we didn't consider how assets moved against each other but instead asked how they moved relative to one factor, such as the stock market, this would reduce the number of parameters required. The beta, β, of an asset measures how sensitive it is to movements in the market. Stocks with betas greater than 1 tend to amplify the overall movements of the market. Stocks with betas between 0 and 1 tend to move in the same direction as the market, but not as far. The market is the portfolio of all stocks and so has a beta of 1.

Some sample betas for S&P 500 companies are given here from 20 October 2017:

Kelloggs[1]	0.21
WAL-MART Stores[2]	0.09
Walt Disney[3]	1.34

---

[1] https://uk.finance.yahoo.com/quote/K?p=K
[2] https://uk.finance.yahoo.com/quote/WMT/?p=WMT
[3] https://uk.finance.yahoo.com/quote/DIS/?p=DIS

Wynn Resorts[4]   2.22

If the stock market rose or fell by 10%, then Kelloggs would rise/fall by 2.1%; Wal-Mart would rise/fall by 0.9%; Walt Disney would rise/fall by 13.4%; and Wynn Resorts would rise/fall by 22.2%.

If an investor expected the stock market to rise they would probably form a portfolio of high-beta (or aggressive) stocks. If on the other hand an investor expected the stock market to fall, they would be more likely to hold low-beta (or defensive) stocks.

The variance (and standard deviation) of a large asset portfolio is given by:

$$\sigma_p^2 = \beta_p^2 \sigma_m^2 \Longrightarrow \sigma_p = \beta_p \sigma_m$$

It follows that the risk of a large, diversified portfolio is directly proportional to the beta of the portfolio. For example, if we formed a large, diversified portfolio with a beta of 1, the standard deviation of the portfolio would be directly proportional to the standard deviation of the market. If, however, we formed a large portfolio with a beta of 1.5, the standard deviation would be 50% higher than the standard deviation of the market.

Betas can be estimated by drawing a scatter diagram, with returns on the stock on the vertical axis and returns on the stock market on the horizontal axis. If we fit a trendline to this scatter diagram, the slope of the line will indicate by what proportion a stock's return changes in response to a given change in the market. When calculating betas it is common practice to use five years of weekly data.

Betas can also be found using the following equation:

$$Beta = \frac{Covariance\ between\ the\ stock\ and\ the\ market}{Variance\ of\ the\ market}$$

---

[4] https://uk.finance.yahoo.com/quote/WYNN/?p=WYNN

Example

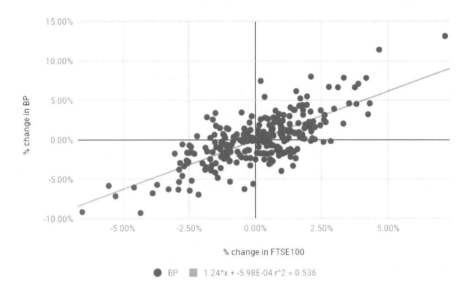

The fitted trendline has an equation of:

$R_{BP} = -0.000598 + 1.24R_m$

Therefore, the beta of BP is 1.24, so a 5% fall in the FTSE100 will lead to a 6.2% fall in the price of BP (1.24 x –5%). The r-squared value indicates that the market risk of BP is 53.6%, with the balance of 46.4% representing unique risk.

Activity 2.2

The spreadsheet available at https://www.liverpooluniversitypress.co.uk/pages/essentials-of-financial-management-efm contains stock price data on Tesla and the S&P500. Please ensure you click on Section 2 and the 2.6 tab at the bottom of the spreadsheet.

Draw a scatter diagram and fit a trendline to fit the beta and market risk for Tesla.

2.7 The capital asset pricing model

The capital asset pricing model (CAPM) was developed by William Sharpe as part of his PhD thesis. He worked partly under the guidance of Harry Markowitz on the topic of "Portfolio Analysis Based on a Simplified Model of the Relationships Among Securities". Important concepts such as the one-factor model and the security market line were developed in this thesis.

The major factor that allowed Markowitz's portfolio theory to develop into capital market theory is the concept of the risk-free asset. A risk-free asset is one with zero variance. By comparison, a risky asset is one for which future returns are uncertain. Recall that covariance between two sets of returns is:

$$\sigma_{ij} = \frac{1}{n}\sum_{i=1}^{n}(R_i - \bar{R_i})\left(R_j - \bar{R_j}\right)$$

where the line (or bar) above R_i and R_j denoted average. It follows that, because the returns for the risk-free asset are certain, $R_i - E(R_i) = 0$, the covariance (and hence correlation) will also be zero.

Once a risk-free rate is introduced, and assuming that "investors are able to borrow or lend funds on equal terms"[5] at the risk-free rate, then we can modify the Markowitz approach as illustrated below:

---

[5] William F. Sharpe, 'Capital asset prices: a theory of market equilibrium under conditions of risk', *The Journal of Finance*, 19.3, (1964), pp. 425–442, p. 433, https://doi.org/10.2307/2977928

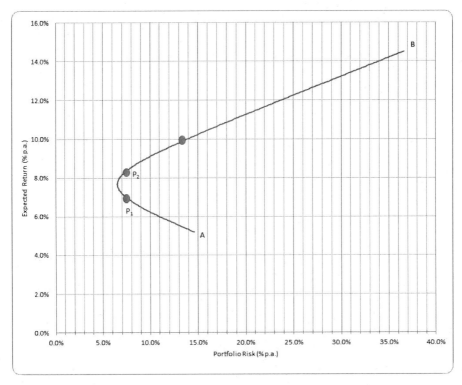

Every combination of the risk-free asset R_f and the market portfolio M is shown on the capital market line (CML). The line is drawn from the vertical axis at the risk-free rate tangential to the Markowitz efficient frontier.

Portfolios to the left of M represent combinations of risky assets and the risk-free asset. Portfolios to the right of M include purchases of risky assets made with funds borrowed at the risk-free rate. Such a portfolio is called a leveraged portfolio.

Compare portfolio P_1 on the Markowitz efficient frontier with portfolio P_2, which is on the CML. Note that for the same level of risk, the expected return is greater for P_2 than for P_1. This is true for all points on the line AB, except portfolio M.

In section 2.4 we concluded that investors will select a portfolio where their indifference curves are tangential to the mean–standard deviation frontier. With the introduction of the risk-free asset, we must now modify this conclusion, such that we now say that an investor will select a portfolio on the line representing a combination of borrowing or lending at the risk-free rate and purchases of the market portfolio, M. The particular efficient portfolio that the investor will select on the line will once again depend on the investor's risk preferences.

The CML is drawn in (total risk, expected return) space. An alternative representation of the CAPM, which recognises that the market only rewards investors for holding market risk, is the security market line (SML). This is drawn in (beta, expected return) space.

Security Market Line

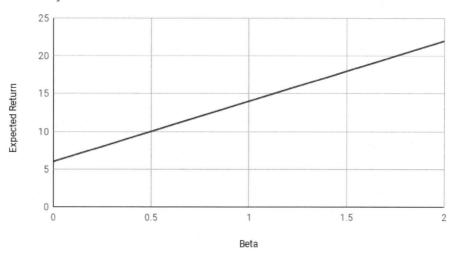

The SML indicates that if your stock (or portfolio) beta is 0, then you will earn the risk-free rate of return. If your stock (or portfolio) beta is 1, then you will earn the same return as the market. If your stock (or portfolio) beta is greater than 1, then you will earn a return in excess of the market.

This SML equation can be expressed algebraically as:

$$E(R_i) = R_f + \beta_i\big[E(R_m) - R_f\big]$$

where

> $E(Ri)$ = expected return on asset I
>
> R_f = the risk-free rate
>
> $E(R_m)$ = expected return on the market
>
> $E(R_m) - R_f$ = market-risk premium

The SML equation states that the expected return on an asset is equal to the risk-free rate plus compensation for market risk represented by the product of the asset's beta and the market-risk premium. The diagram and the algebraic representation confirm that the relationship between expected returns is a linear one, and the higher the level of systematic risk, the greater the expected return.

When beta = 0:

$$E(R_i) = R_f + 0 \times \left[E(R_m) - R_f\right] = R_f$$

When beta = 1:

$$E(R_i) = R_f + 1 \times \left[E(R_m) - R_f\right] = E(R_m)$$

Example

Let the risk-free rate be 2%. Suppose the rate of return of the market has an expected value of 12% and a standard deviation of 15%. Now consider an asset that has a covariance of 0.045 with the market. What is the expected return of the asset?

First of all we need to find the beta:

$\beta = 0.045/.15^2 = 0.045/0.0225 = 2$

Now plug the values into the SML equation:

$E(R_i) = 0.02 + 2\ [0.12 - 0.02] = 0.02 + 2 \times 0.1 = 0.12 = 12\%$

In equilibrium, we assume that all stocks lie on the SML and that any temporary deviations will be exploited through the activities of arbitrageurs whose actions will return the stock to the SML.

Consider two securities, HSL and PJL, which lie on the security market line.

Security	HSL	PJL
Beta	1	1.5
Expected return	14%	18%

As we have two points on the SML we can obtain its equation. Using the standard form of the equation of a straight line, y = ax + b, and inserting the coordinates (1, 14) and (1.5, 18):

14 = a x 1 + b

18 = a x 1.5 + b

Subtracting the first equation from the second:

4 = a (0.5) therefore a = 8

In this context, a represents the risk-free rate.

Substituting in the first equation:

b = 14 − 8 x 1 = 6

In this context, b represents the market-risk premium. As HSL has a beta of 1 and a return of 14%, then given that the risk-free rate was found to be 8%, we could immediately infer that the market risk premium was 6% (i.e. 14% − 8%).

The equation of the SML is then:

$$E(R_i) = 8 + 6\beta_i$$

Consider now the security MGL, which has a beta of 1.8 and is priced to give an expected return of 24%. According to the SML, the expected return should be:

$$E(R_i) = 8 + 6\beta_i = 8 + 6 \times 1.8 = 20.4\%$$

Therefore MGL is priced to give an expected return that is higher than that predicted by the SML. This is represented by the red dot on the diagram below.

The security KAL, which has a beta of 0.5, is priced to give an expected return of 8%. According to the SML, the expected return should be:

$$E(R_i) = 8 + 6\beta_i = 8 + 6 \times 0.5 = 11\%$$

Therefore KAL is priced to give an expected return that is lower than that predicted by the SML. This is represented by the yellow dot on the diagram below.

Security Market Line

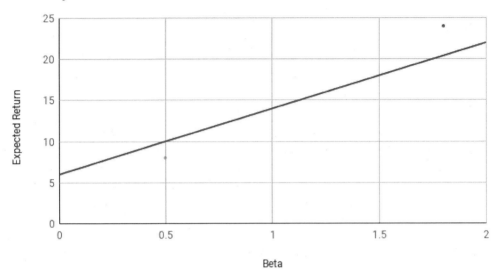

Is MGL over-priced or under-priced? The temptation is to say over-priced, as it lies above the SML. However, the SML is drawn in (beta, expected return) space not (beta, price) space, and in fact MGL is under-priced. As arbitrageurs realise this and buy the asset, market forces will force the price up, and as investors are now buying the asset at a higher price, the expected return will fall. It will continue to fall until it is commensurate with the degree of market risk.

In comparison, KAL lies below the SML and is over-priced. The actions of arbitrageurs selling this security will force the price down, and hence the expected return will rise until KAL lies on the SML.

A key feature of the CAPM is beta, which can be found using:

$$Beta = \frac{Covariance\ between\ the\ stock\ and\ the\ market}{Variance\ of\ the\ market}$$

Therefore in order to calculate beta we need to identify the market portfolio. It is commonly accepted that "the market portfolio is defined as a value-weighted combination of all assets".[6] In practice no such portfolio exists that represents all potential assets. To circumvent this problem many researchers use share indices, such as the S&P500 or the FTSE100, as a proxy for the market portfolio. In fact, in example 2.2 above, we have also used a proxy in order to calculate the beta. Roll argues that "[CAPM] theory is not testable unless the exact composition of the true market portfolio is known and used in the tests. This implies that the theory is not testable unless all individual assets are included in the sample."[7] This is known as "Roll's critique".

2.8 The beta of a portfolio

For a portfolio of N assets, the portfolio beta is found using:

$$\beta_p = \sum_{i=1}^{N} \omega_i \beta_i$$

i.e. a weighted average of all of the betas in the portfolio. For example, if I held 50% of my wealth in stock A, and 50% of my wealth in stock B, which have betas of 1.5 and 2 respectively, then the beta of my portfolio would be:

0.5 x 1.5 + 0.5 x 2 = 1.75

Hence, if the market rose by 10% then stock A would rise by 15% and stock B by 20%. The net effect on the portfolio would be a rise of 17.5%.

Activity 2.3

You own 10,000 shares in Ford (beta = 1.31, price = US$12.10), 10,000 in Verizon (beta = 0.71, price = US$49.53) and 10,000 in Proctor and Gamble (beta = 0.52, price = US$88.55).

What is the beta of your portfolio?

---

[6] Richard Roll, 'A critique of the asset pricing theory's tests Part I: On past and potential testability of the theory', *Journal of Financial Economics*, 4.2 (1977), pp. 129–176, p. 137.
[7] Roll, 'A critique of the asset pricing theory's tests Part I', p. 130.

Harry Markowitz, William Sharpe and Merton Miller received the Nobel Prize for Economics in 1990 for their contributions to portfolio theory. A discussion of their contribution can be found on the Nobel Prize website.[8]

---

[8] https://www.nobelprize.org/nobel_prizes/economic-sciences/laureates/1990/press.html

3

The time value of money, the dividend discount model and dividend policy

3.1 The time value of money

Ask your friends how much money they would need to be offered in one year's time to make them indifferent between that amount and a guaranteed £1,000 now. The answer will vary from individual to individual, and will also vary geographically.

Any rational individual will prefer certain money now rather than uncertain money in the future. This is known as the "time value of money". Even though you do not realise it, when answering the question above, you are implicitly thinking about important concepts such as opportunity cost, inflation and risk. For example, by how much are prices rising, how much satisfaction you would gain from spending the money now and what is the likelihood of the future payment not occurring? In order to determine the future amount that will make us indifferent, an investor will require compensation for these three elements.

The eagerness to spend the £1,000 now is the most difficult to quantify, but for inflation and risk it is easy to assign numerical values. Assume that inflation is 5% p.a. and we attach an amount of 3% to the eagerness to consume. In order to reward an investor for these two factors the required return would need to be:

$(1 + 0.05) \times (1 + 0.03) - 1 = 8.15\%$

The closest investment we have that simply rewards investors for loss of consumption and inflation, with no risk, is a short-term government security. In Chapter 2 we referred to such an asset as the risk-free rate.

However, physical investments such as building an office block or manufacturing a new product, and financial investments such as buying shares or bonds, carry with them a degree of risk. Investors therefore demand a "risk premium" beyond the risk-free rate when making investments with uncertain outcomes. We have already seen in section 2.7 that when determining the expected return on an asset we use the security market line:

$$E(R_i) = R_f + \beta_i \big[E(R_m) - R_f \big]$$

More generally we can write:

required return = risk-free rate + risk premium

Therefore, when we are attempting to compare different amounts of money at different points in time, we need to take into consideration the eagerness to spend, inflation and risk.

3.2 Present values

Many topics in finance, including investment appraisal/NPV analysis, bond pricing and the dividend discount model, to take three examples, have the time value of money at their very heart.

In order to compare like with like, it is important to value cash flows at the same point in time, which might be the current time period or some time period in the future. In order to measure cash flows at a particular point in time we use a tool called "discounted cash flow". In section 3.1, we assumed a risk-free rate of 8.15%. If the risk premium was a further 10%, then the future value of £1,000 could be calculated as follows:

£1000 x $(1 + 0.0815)^1$ = £1,081.5

Given these assumptions, a rational investor would be indifferent between £1,000 now and £1,081.50 in the future. Here, we have found the future value of an amount P (here £1,000) at a discount rate of r, in t years' time.

future value = P x $(1+ r)^t$

It is more common to consider a future cash flow, CF_t (e.g. a dividend payment or a coupon from a bond), and find its present value:

$$Present\ Value = \frac{CF_t}{(1+r)^t}$$

Here, we are said to have taken some future cash flow and discounted it back to time zero.

More formally, in order to find the present value of some future cash flow, we multiply the cash flow by the discount factor:

$$DF = \frac{1}{(1+r)^t}$$

$$PV = DF \times C_t = \frac{C_t}{(1+r)^t}$$

where C_t is the cash flow received in time period t, and r is the required return/time value of money.

Present values (PV) can be added together to evaluate multiple cash flows:

$$PV = \frac{C_1}{(1+r)^1} + \frac{C_2}{(1+r)^2} + \frac{C_3}{(1+r)^3} + \dots$$

Each individual cash flow is measured in "year zero" money and therefore can be added together, which is the additive property of discount cash flow. It is evident from the equation above that the greater r is, the higher the denominator, hence the lower the discount factor and consequently the lower the PV. In addition, the further into the future is the cash flow, the higher the denominator, the lower the discount factor and the lower the PV.

Example

    i.   What is the PV of a cash flow of $100 received in one year's time at discount rate of 5%?

    ii. What is the PV of a cash flow of $100 received in 10 years' time at discount rate of 5%?

    iii. What is the PV of a cash flow of $100 received in 10 years' time at discount rate of 20%?

(i) $PV = \frac{\$100}{(1+0.05)^1} = \$95.24$

(ii) $PV = \frac{\$100}{(1+0.05)^{10}} = \$61.39$

(iii) $PV = \frac{\$100}{(1+0.20)^{10}} = \$16.15$

The table below shows how the PV of $100 varies with r and t.

CF	$100						
T/r	1%	2%	5%	10%	15%	20%	50%
1	$99.01	$98.04	$95.24	$90.91	$86.96	$83.33	$66.67
2	$98.03	$96.12	$90.70	$82.64	$75.61	$69.44	$44.44
3	$97.06	$94.23	$86.38	$75.13	$65.75	$57.87	$29.63
4	$96.10	$92.38	$82.27	$68.30	$57.18	$48.23	$19.75
5	$95.15	$90.57	$78.35	$62.09	$49.72	$40.19	$13.17
6	$94.20	$88.80	$74.62	$56.45	$43.23	$33.49	$8.78
7	$93.27	$87.06	$71.07	$51.32	$37.59	$27.91	$5.85
8	$92.35	$85.35	$67.68	$46.65	$32.69	$23.26	$3.90
9	$91.43	$83.68	$64.46	$42.41	$28.43	$19.38	$2.60
10	$90.53	$82.03	$61.39	$38.55	$24.72	$16.15	$1.73

From the above you can see that at a rate of interest of 50% p.a., the present value of $100 received in 10 years' time is just $1.73.

3.3 Perpetuities and annuities

Perpetuities and annuities are two special cases that we must consider. An annuity is an investment that pays a fixed sum each year for a specified number of years. In contrast, a perpetuity is a financial concept in which a cash flow is theoretically received forever. In Chapter 1 you were introduced to preference shares, a type of share that pays a fixed dividend forever.

The value of a perpetuity can be found by:

$$Present\ Value\ of\ a\ Perpetuty = \frac{Cash\ Flow}{discount\ rate}$$

For example, the value of an asset that promises to pay $100 forever, where the required return is 5% p.a., is:

$$PV\ of\ Cash\ Flow = \frac{\$100}{0.05} = \$2000$$

This asset could be, for example, a preference share. If the preference share paid a fixed dividend of $100 per annum, and the market viewed the risk of these cash flows to be 5% p.a., then the market value of the preference share would be $2,000. It is evident that as r increases, the value of the preference share will fall. The example below illustrates how, given the dividend and value of a preference share, we can find the discount rate used by the market to arrive at this price.

A 10% UK preference share pays out 10% of a nominal value of 100 pence forever, i.e. it pays out 10p per annum. The price observed in the market is therefore the present value of 10p at a discount rate, which the market views as representing the risk inherent in the future cash flows. It follows then that if we observe the price of the preference share to be 120p, then the market must have used:

$$Preference\ Share\ Price = \frac{Preference\ Dividend}{r} \rightarrow r$$

$$= \frac{Preference\ Dividend}{Preference\ Share\ Price}$$

$$= \frac{10}{120} = 8.33\%$$

It follows that the price of preference shares varies with the market's view of the riskiness of the future cash flows. For example, following the *Deepwater Horizon* oil rig disaster in April 2010, the price of 8% BP preference shares fell from around 160 pence to 125 pence. The reason for the drop was that the market felt that the riskiness of future cash flows had risen from 5% (= 8/160) to 6.4% (= 8/125).

The value of an annuity can be found using:

$$PV\ of\ annuity = C \times \left[\frac{1}{r} - \frac{1}{r(1+r)^t} \right]$$

The term in brackets is referred to as the annuity factor.

For example, if an investment pays $100 each year for 20 years and the discount rate is assumed to be 5% p.a., then the value of this investment is:

$$PV\ of\ annuity = C \times \left[\frac{1}{r} - \frac{1}{r(1+r)^t} \right] = \$100 \times \left[\frac{1}{0.05} - \frac{1}{0.05(1+0.05)^{20}} \right] = \$1,246.22$$

The working out is detailed below:

C	$100
r	5%
t	20
1/r	20
r(1+r)^t	0.1327
1/(r(1+r)^t)	7.5378
Annuity factor	12.4622
PV	**$1,246.22**

Alternatively, in Excel, =-pv(0.05,20,100) would have also generated the answer of $1,246,22.

Activity 3.1

Visit the website of the London Stock Exchange[1] and search for "BP.A". This is a British Petroleum 8% preference share. Display the chart over the last five years and determine the lowest share price and the highest share price. What discount rate was the market using to arrive at these values?

At the time of writing (October 2017), the annuity rate quoted for a single 55-year-old living in London was £4,216. What this figure represents is how much annual income could be purchased with £100,000. Recall that to find the present value of an annuity we need to know the values for r and t, where t in this context will represent life expectancy. The Office of National Statistics maintains a database of UK life expectancy according to age and gender which, based on data for the years 2014–16, is presently 24.82 years (for a male aged 55).

If interest rates were 5%, then the PV of £1 received for the next 24.82 years would be:

$$\text{PV of annuity} = C \times \left[\frac{1}{r} - \frac{1}{r(1+r)^t}\right] = £1 \times \left[\frac{1}{0.05} - \frac{1}{0.05(1+0.05)^{26.82}}\right] = £14.5958$$

---

[1] http://www.londonstockexchange.com/

Hence if £100,000 was available to buy an annuity, this would be quoted as:

£100,000/£14.5958 = £6,851.29

In order to find the discount rate used to arrive at an answer of £4,216 we would need to discount cash flows at a lower r:

C	£1.00
r	0.905%
t	26.82
1/r	110.5219135
r(1+r)^t	0.0115
1/(r(1+r)^t)	86.8027
Annuity factor	**23.7192**
PV	£23.7192

Investment	**£100,000.00**
Annuity rate	**£4,215.99**

3.4 Dividend discount model

For security analysts and portfolio managers it could be very useful to compute the "equilibrium" price of a security. This value would be especially important if analysts believed that any deviations of the actual price from the theoretical price would only be temporary, so that they could buy temporarily cheap securities and sell temporarily expensive ones. Clearly such strategies are relevant if prices have a tendency to converge towards their fundamental values.

The dividend discount model is based on the premise that the market value of ordinary shares represents the sum of expected future dividends, to infinity, discounted to time zero.

Consider a shareholder who intends to hold a share for one year. A single dividend will be paid at the end of the holding period, d_1, and the share will be sold at a price p_1 in one year. To derive the value of a share at time 0 to this investor, the future cash flows d_1 and p_1 need to be discounted at a rate which includes an allowance for the risk of the share, k:

$$p_0 = \frac{d_1}{1+k} + \frac{p_1}{1+k}$$

Consider a second investor who expects to hold the share for a further year and sell at time 2 for p_2; the price, p_1, will be:

$$p_1 = \frac{d_2}{1+k} + \frac{p_2}{1+k}$$

Substituting into the equation for p_0 we get:

$$p_0 = \frac{d_1}{1+k} + \frac{d_2}{(1+k)^2} + \frac{p_2}{(1+k)^2}$$

If a series of one-year investors bought this share, and we in turn solved for p_2, p_3 etc., we would find:

$$p_0 = \frac{d_1}{1+k} + \frac{d_2}{(1+k)^2} + ... \frac{d_\infty}{(1+k)^\infty}$$

The terminal stock price can effectively be ignored as its present value is zero. However, its value feeds into $p_{\infty-1}$ etc. and so by iteration it enters into p_0.

The above model is called the dividend discount model (DDM) and can be written, using sigma notation, as:

$$P_t = \sum_{t=1}^{\infty} \frac{d_{t+1}}{(1+k)^t}$$

Consider stock A that has just paid a dividend of $10 and is expected to pay this dividend forever. If the cost of capital, k, is 5%, what is the value of stock A?

We could use Excel and find the PV and the future dividends and sum them together, as follows:

k	5%		
Year	Div	PV(Div)	Sum (years 1 – 500) = $200
1	$10.00	$9.52	
2	$10.00	$9.07	
3	$10.00	$8.64	
4	$10.00	$8.23	
5	$10.00	$7.84	
6	$10.00	$7.46	
7	$10.00	$7.11	

k	5%		
Year	Div	PV(Div)	Sum (years 1 – 500) = $200
8	$10.00	$6.77	
9	$10.00	$6.45	
10	$10.00	$6.14	

Or alternatively we could treat this as a perpetuity and find the price directly using $10/0.05 = $200.

The spreadsheet for this exercise can be found at https://www.liverpooluniversitypress.co.uk/pages/essentials-of-financial-management-efm. Please ensure you click on Section 3 and the 3.4a tab at the bottom of the spreadsheet.

Note, at a discount rate of 5%, it takes 156 years in order for the PV to drop below 1 cent.

Consider stock B that will not pay a dividend for the next five years, but in year six will pay a dividend of $10 and is expected to pay this dividend forever. If the cost of capital, k, is 5%, what is the value of stock B? Again, we can map out the future dividends in Excel, find the PVs and sum them together.

k	5%		
Year	Div	PV(Div)	Sum (years 1 – 500) = $156.71
1	$0.00	$0.00	
2	$0.00	$0.00	
3	$0.00	$0.00	
4	$0.00	$0.00	
5	$0.00	$0.00	
6	$10.00	$7.46	
7	$10.00	$7.11	
8	$10.00	$6.77	
9	$10.00	$6.45	
10	$10.00	$6.14	

The spreadsheet for this exercise can be found at https://www.liverpooluniversitypress.co.uk/pages/essentials-of-financial-management-efm. Please ensure you click on Section 3 and the 3.4b tab at the bottom of the spreadsheet.

Clearly the answer is lower than that of Stock A. We could have found the answer by taking the value of Stock A and subtracting the sum of the PVs from years 1 to 5 (in fact this is an annuity, for which there is a formula). Or we can think laterally ...

Figuratively speaking, standing at the end of year 5 we know that Stock B will pay a dividend of $10 and pay this dividend forever. In "year five money" the value of Stock B is:

$P_5 = \$10/0.05 = \$200$

In order to get the value in "year zero money" we need to discount at 5% over five years:

$P_0 = \$200/1.055 = \$156.71$

3.5 The Gordon growth model

According to the dividend discount model, the equilibrium price of a share is equal to the sum of future dividends, discounted at an appropriate rate of interest to time 0:

$$P_t = \sum_{t=1}^{\infty} \frac{d_{t+1}}{(1+k)^t}$$

This model works fine for preference shares, where dividends are known, but for ordinary shares it is less effective. Instead we have to view the equilibrium share price as the sum of the present value of expected future dividends.

$$P_t = \sum_{t=1}^{\infty} E_{t=0} \left[\frac{d_t}{(1+k)^t} \right]$$

That is, the equilibrium share price is the sum of the present value of expected future dividends, with the expectation formed at time 0. In order to overcome the issue of forming expectations, Myron J. Gordon (1962)[2] simplified the problem by assuming that dividends grow at some rate g, each year.

To motivate the model let us use the following notation:

d_t = the last dividend paid by the company

$d_{t+1} = d_t \times (1 + g)$

---

[2] Myron J. Gordon, *The Investment, Financing, and Valuation of the Corporation* (Homewood, III, R.D. Iriwn, 1962).

It follows that the expectation made at time t (i.e. year 0) for the dividend received in period 2 is:

$$E_t(d_{t+2}) = d_{t+1} \times (1+g)$$

And the expectation made at time t (i.e. year 0) for the dividend received in period 3 is:

$$E_t(d_{t+3}) = E_t(d_{t+2}) \times (1+g) = d_{t+1} \times (1+g)^2$$

Hence the expectation made at time t (i.e. year 0) for the dividend received in period i is:

$$E_t(d_{t+i}) = d_{t+1} \times (1+g)^{i-1}$$

Substituting this result into the generic dividend discount model:

$$P_t = \sum_{t=1}^{\infty} E_{t=0}\left[\frac{d_t}{(1+k)^t}\right] = \sum_{t=1}^{\infty} \frac{d_{t+1}(1+g)^{t-1}}{(1+k)^t}$$

Consider stock C that has just paid a dividend of $10 and is expected to grow dividends at 2% forever. If the cost of capital, k, is 5% what is the value of stock C? Again, we can map out the future dividends in Excel, find the PVs and sum them together.

d_t	$10.00	$g = 2\%$	$d_t + 1 = \$10.20$
k	5%		
Year	Div	PV(Div)	Sum (years 1 – 500) = $340.00
1	$10.20	$9.71	
2	$10.40	$9.44	
3	$10.61	$9.17	
4	$10.82	$8.91	
5	$11.04	$8.65	
6	$11.26	$8.40	
7	$11.49	$8.16	
8	$11.72	$7.93	
9	$11.95	$7.70	
10	$12.19	$7.48	

Clearly the answer is larger than stock A ($200) as dividends are growing by 2% each year.

The spreadsheet for this exercise can be found at https://www.liverpooluniversitypress.co.uk/pages/essentials-of-financial-management-efm. Please ensure you click on Section 3 and the 3.5 tab at the bottom of the spreadsheet.

It is not particularly practical to implement this approach without a spreadsheet. But with some algebraic manipulation we can arrive at a simple equation.

$$P_t = \sum_{t=1}^{\infty} \frac{d_{t+1}(1+g)^{t-1}}{(1+k)^t}$$

If we can get the summation sign from zero to infinity rather than from 1 to infinity, we can treat the result as a geometric series. Note, if we start summing from 1 we must increase the index within the summation by 1 to give:

$$P_t = \sum_{t=0}^{\infty} \frac{d_{t+1}(1+g)^t}{(1+k)^{t+1}}$$

Note that we can remove the d_{t+1}, from the summation as it does not have an "i" index and we can simplify further:

$$P_t = d_{t+1} \sum_{t=0}^{\infty} \frac{(1+g)^t}{(1+k)^{t+1}} = d_{t+1} \sum_{t=0}^{\infty} \frac{(1+g)^t}{(1+k)^t(1+k)}$$

$$P_t = \frac{d_{t+1}}{(1+k)} \sum_{t=0}^{\infty} \frac{(1+g)^t}{(1+k)^t} = \frac{d_{t+1}}{(1+k)} \sum_{t=0}^{\infty} \left(\frac{1+g}{1+k}\right)^t$$

The last expression on the right-hand side is a geometric expression. If $g < k$ so that the entire bracketed term < 1, we can use the following rule:

$$\sum_{i=0}^{\infty} a^i = \frac{1}{1-a} \quad \text{if } a < 1$$

Then:

$$P_t = \frac{d_{t+1}}{(1+k)} \times \frac{1}{1 - \left(\frac{1+g}{1+k}\right)} = \frac{d_{t+1}}{k-g}$$

i.e. the equilibrium share price is the next period dividend divided by k minus g. For Stock C:

Pt = $10 x 1.02/(0.05 – 0.03) = $10.2/0.02 = $340.

Example

Stock A is expected to pay a dividend of £10 forever.

Stock B is expected to pay a dividend of £8 next year, with dividend growth expected to be 3% per annum thereafter.

Stock C just paid a dividend of £6 with dividend growth expected to be 4% p.a. thereafter.

If the required return on similar equities is 10%, calculate the value of each stock.

Solution

A: £10/0.1 = £100

B: £8/(0.1 − 0.03) = £8/0.07 = £114.29

C: (£6 x 1.04)/(0.1 − 0.04) = £6.24/0.06 = £104

3.6 Two-period dividend growth model

What if we do not anticipate a constant rate of growth of dividends? In this case we would need to forecast all future dividend payments, which is of course impossible. One solution is to assume that dividends grow at a constant rate over a certain period and then grow at a different rate over a second period etc. Clearly the simplest case to solve is the two-period growth model in which dividends grow at g_1 in periods 1 to N and then at g_2 in periods N +1 to infinity. This is best illustrated by way of an example.

Consider stock D that has just paid a dividend of $10 and is expected to maintain this stable dividend for the next five years, and then grow dividends at 2% forever. If the cost of capital, k, is 5%, what is the value of stock D? Again, we can map out the future dividends in Excel, find the PVs and sum them together.

d_t	$10.00	$g_1 = 0\%$	$d_t + 1 = \$10.00$
k	5%	$g_2 = 2\%$	N = 5
Year	Div	PV(Div)	Sum (years 1 – 500) = $309.69
1	$10.00	$9.52	
2	$10.00	$9.07	
3	$10.00	$8.64	Sum = $43.29
4	$10.00	$8.23	
5	$10.00	$7.84	
6	$10.20	$7.61	
7	$10.40	$7.39	
8	$10.61	$7.18	

9	$10.82	$6.98
10	$11.04	$6.78

Clearly the answer is larger than stock A ($200), as dividends are growing by 2% each year, but less than stock C, as growth was delayed until the sixth year.

The spreadsheet for this exercise can be found at https://www.liverpooluniversitypress.co.uk/pages/essentials-of-financial-management-efm. Please ensure you click on Section 3 and the 3.6a tab at the bottom of the spreadsheet.

Once again it is not particularly practical to implement this approach without a spreadsheet. However, with some lateral thinking it is possible to solve the problem easily.

In "year five money" the value of Stock D's cash flows in year 6 and beyond is:

$P_5 = (\$10 \times 1.02)/(0.05-0.02) = \$340$

In order to get the value in "year zero money" we need to discount at 5% over five years:

$P_0 = \$340/1.05^5 = \$266.40$

But then, of course, we have to consider the PV of the dividends received in years 1 to 5:

1	$10.00	$9.52	
2	$10.00	$9.07	
3	$10.00	$8.64	Sum = $43.29
4	$10.00	$8.23	
5	$10.00	$7.84	

giving a total of $266.40 + $43.29 = $309.69.

More formally we can determine the dividend in each period as:

$d_{t+1} = d_t(1 + g_1)$

$E_t(d_{t+2}) = d_{t+1}(1 + g_1)$

$E_t(d_{t+3}) = E_t(d_{t+2})(1 + g_1) = d_{t+1}(1 + g_1)^2$

$E_t(d_{t+N}) = E_t(d_{t+N-1})(1 + g_1) = d_{t+1}(1 + g1)^{N-1}$

$\ldots$

$E_t(d_{t+N+1}) = E_t(d_{t+N})(1 + g_2) = d_{t+1}(1 + g_1)^{N-1}(1 + g_2)$

$E_t(d_{t+N+2}) = E_t(d_{t+N+1})(1 + g_2) = d_{t+1}(1 + g_1)^{N-1}(1 + g_2)^2$

$\ldots$

$E_t(d_{t+N+i}) = d_{t+1}(1 + g_1)^{N-1}(1 + g_2)^i$

In the example above, $d_t = \$10$, $g_1 = 0\%$ (therefore $d_{t+1} = \$10$), $g_2 = 2\%$ and $N = 5$. Therefore the dividend, in say period 8, can be found using:

$E_t(D_{t+N+i}) = d_{t+1}(1 + g_1)^{N-1}(1 + g_2)^i = E_t(d_{t+5+3}) = \$10 \times (1 + 0)^4 \times (1 + 0.02)^3 = \$10.61$

Consider stock E that has just paid a dividend of $10 and is expected to grow this dividend at a rate of 10% p.a. for the next five years, and then grow dividends at 2% forever. If the cost of capital, k, is 5%, what is the value of stock E?

Again, we can map out the future dividends in Excel, find the PVs and sum them together.

d_t	$10.00	$g_1 = 10\%$	$d_t + 1 = 11.00$
k	5%	$g_2 = 2\%$	N = 5
Year	Div	PV(Div)	Sum (years 1 – 500) = $486.65
1	$11.00	$10.48	
2	$12.10	$10.98	
3	$13.31	$11.50	$57.61
4	$14.64	$12.05	
5	$16.11	$12.62	
6	$16.43	$12.26	
7	$16.76	$11.91	
8	$17.09	$11.57	
9	$17.43	$11.24	
10	$17.78	$10.92	

Here, we map out the dividends in the "finite" period of years 1–5 as above and find the PV to be $57.61. Next, we move to year 5 where the dividend is expected to be $16.11 after five years of growth at 10%. The dividend in period 6 is then:

$\$16.11 \times 1.02 = \$16.43$

Using the single-period growth model, the value of the cash flows in year 6 and beyond (in year 5 money) is then:

$\$16.43/(0.05 - 0.02) = \$547.67$

In order to compare this to the $57.61 figure obtained earlier, we need to discount these cash flows back to year 0:

$$\$547.67/(1 + 0.05)^5 = \$ 429.11$$

The value of stock E is then $57.61 + $429.11 = $486.72. Note that the slight discrepancy in the answer above is due to rounding.

The spreadsheet for this exercise can be found at https://www.liverpooluniversitypress.co.uk/pages/essentials-of-financial-management-efm. Please ensure you click on Section 3 and the 3.6b tab at the bottom of the spreadsheet.

3.7 Example with earnings growth

Vornado is a company that has patent rights for a new mobile phone technology that is expected to enable it to generate growth in earnings of 20% for the next three years. After that (from the start of year 4) the company expects to see earnings growth drop to a constant rate of 5%. Assuming that the company pays out 60% of earnings as dividends and that the last dividend payment made by the company was $2.20, calculate an estimate of the current price of Vornado. Assume that the required return on equity is 8%.

This is rather a difficult exercise as it has a number of complexities relative to previous examples. Was the reference to the company paying out 60% of earnings as dividends and growing earnings by 20% a "red herring"? Let's assume some earnings and share values.

Year 0

Earnings = $3,666,666.67

Number of shares = 1,000,000

What is the total dividend and the dividend per share?

Dividend = 60% x $3,666,666.67 = $2,200,000

Dividend per share = $2.20

Note we arrive at the same answer if the number of shares is 500,000 and the earnings are $1,833,333.33.

If the firm grows earnings at 20% per annum, then the new earnings level, total dividend and dividend per share are as follows:

Year 1

Earnings= $4,400,000.00,

Dividends = $2,640,000.00

Dividend per share= $2.64

Dividends have increased from $2.20 to $2.64, which is an increase of [$2.64 − $2.20]/$2.20 = 20%

Hence, if a firm is to pay a constant proportion of earnings, then earnings growth and dividend growth are the same. For example:

$$DPS_0 = \frac{c \times Earnings}{n}$$

$$DPS_1 = \frac{c \times Earnings \times (1 + g)}{n}$$

$$\frac{DPS_1 - DPS_0}{DPS_0} = \frac{\frac{c \times Earnings \times (1+g)}{n} - \frac{c \times Earnings}{n}}{\frac{c \times Earnings}{n}}$$

$$\frac{DPS_1 - DPS_0}{DPS_0} = \frac{\frac{c \times Earnings}{n}[1 + g - 1]}{\frac{c \times Earnings}{n}} = g$$

The case can now be expressed as:

Vornado is a company that has patent rights for a new mobile phone technology that is expected to enable it to generate growth in DIVIDENDS of 20% for the next three years. After that (from the start of year 4) the company expects to see DIVIDENDS' growth drop to a constant rate of 5%. The last dividend payment made by the company was $2.20; calculate an estimate of the current price of Vornado. Assume the required return on equity is 8%.

Now we need to map out the future stream of dividends:

Year	Dividend
1	$2.64
2	$2.64 + 20% = $3.17
3	$3.17 + 20% = $3.80
4	$3.80 + 5% = $3.99

In year 4, dividend growth drops to 5% and continues to grow at 5% into infinity.

Finding the sum over the first three periods is trivial:

$2.64/1.08 + $3.17/1.08^2 + $3.80/1.08^3 = $8.18.

In order to find the value of the dividends beyond period 3 we need to use the Gordon growth model:

$3.99/(0.08 – 0.05) = $133

However, that is in "year 3 money", and so to find the value now we must find its present value (PV):

$133.00/1.08^3 = $105.58

Adding this to the PV of the dividends from years 1 to 3 we get a current share price of:

$8.18 + $105.58 = $113.76

3.8 Real-life dividend policy

The fact that corporations and shareholders expend a considerable amount of energy on analysing a corporation's dividend policy suggests that dividend payments have a significant effect on the share price or value of the company. It was therefore surprising that in 1961 Modigliani and Miller published an article, "Dividend Policy, Growth, and the Valuation of Shares",[3] which demonstrated that in certain circumstances a corporation's decision regarding its dividend payments would have no effect on the value of its shares. Prior to this article, it was widely accepted that the more dividends a firm paid, the higher would be its value, as we see in the dividend discount model.

There have been a number of arguments proposed to explain why dividends might be relevant. Below we outline three of these.

1. **Tax and clientele effect.** In many countries, the investor receiving dividends is taxed at a higher rate than the investor who obtains a capital gain by selling shares. Hence investors might prefer to receive their share of the firm's profit in the form of a capital gain rather than in the form of a dividend. Moreover, even if realised capital gains and dividends incur the same tax rate, investors may prefer a firm not to pay a dividend because, although that would lead to a higher share price, the investor can postpone tax by delaying the sale of the share. This is because tax is charged on capital gains only when the share is sold and the capital gain realised, so the investor is able to postpone tax liability and benefit from retaining the use of the tax funds. In contrast, tax on dividend income cannot be postponed. Therefore dividend policy is not irrelevant, and firms have an incentive not to pay dividends so as to help their shareholders avoid taxation. In reality, however, investors are taxed differently and the fact that investors are subject to different taxes can lead to their forming clienteles

---

[3] Merton H. Miller and Franco Modigliani, 'Dividend policy, growth, and the valuation of shares', *The Journal of Business*, 34.4 (1961), pp. 411–433.

based on their tax bracket. Investors in high tax brackets invest in stock with low dividend payouts, while those in low tax brackets invest in high-dividend-paying stocks. The gravitation of investors towards companies with dividend policies more suited to their own individual tax situations is often referred to as the "clientele effect". Tax clienteles are different types of shareholders, each preferring a specific kind of dividend policy due to differences in their tax brackets. The clientele effect suggests that with diverse investors, the value of the firm is independent of its payout policy. If a firm increases its dividend payout, it may lose some shareholders, but then other investors, who prefer this new dividend policy, will replace them.

2. **Clientele effect again.** It can be further argued that an investor's attraction to a company will depend on their current financial situation. For example, if an investor has more than enough money from their paid employment and would probably only reinvest dividend income in the stock market, then they will be attracted to stocks with a low dividend payout rate/high reinvestment rate. In comparison, an investor who relies on dividend income to live on would be attracted to stocks with a high dividend payout rate. Pension funds, which need regular income, would also be attracted to such stocks. Interestingly, the dividend discount models outlined above rely on the fact that companies pay a dividend. Apple, for example, did not pay a dividend from December 1995 to August 2012. In contrast, British American Tobacco grows its annual dividend year on year.

Date	BAT annual dividend
1999	20.3
2000	26.9
2001	29.7
2002	33
2003	36.3
2004	39.7
2005	43.2
2006	48.7
2007	58.8
2008	69.7
2009	99.5
2010	114.2
2011	126.5
2012	130.6
2013	142.4

2014	148.1
2015	150
2016	155.9
2017	174.6

In percentage terms British American Tobacco has grown the dividend by:

$$g = \sqrt[18]{\frac{174.6}{20.3}} - 1 = 12.70\% \text{ per annum.}$$

3. **Asymmetric information.** The Modigliani–Miller "dividend irrelevance" result was derived within a model of perfectly competitive markets, including the assumption that there is perfect information – that financial investors (shareholders) and managers have the same, freely available information on which to base their valuation of the corporation. This does not mean that variables are known with complete certainty, but the point is that all parties have the same knowledge of those uncertain variables. In reality, however, shareholders and managers may have different degrees of knowledge about the corporation. It follows that when shareholders have imperfect information, managers can choose to use dividends as a signal to convey information about the company. Therefore, if information is asymmetric, a company could try and convey confidence about the future to financial markets, which it could do by increasing the dividend beyond the increase expected by the market. In contrast, if the firm chose to reduce the dividend it would convey a negative signal about its future prospects. Consequently, dividends can affect the value of the corporation by influencing shareholders' perception and valuation of its prospects and risks; consequently, the choice of dividend policy does matter.

Activity 3.2

Search online for the following terms: "Investor relations Amazon", "Investor relations Alphabet" and "Investor relations Imperial Brands" and obtain the most recent annual reports. Search the annual report (CTRL + F) for the word "dividend". What is the dividend policy for each of these companies?

4

The valuation of bonds

4.1 Introduction to bonds

A bond is an instrument issued by a company (corporate bond), a country (sovereign debt) or a state/city (municipal bond). They have a finite life, and may make a periodic payment (a coupon) and some final payment (par value). Bonds that do not make a periodic payment are known as zero coupon bonds.

In order to evaluate the price of a bond we need to sum together the present value of future cash flows, evaluated at some required rate of return that reflects the riskiness of those flows. This technique is near identical to the dividend discount model, with a number of noticeable differences:

1. bonds have a finite life; shares are irredeemable and hence have an infinite life

2. bond payments (coupon and par value) are known with certainty, whereas dividends paid on ordinary shares are uncertain

4.2 Bond pricing

Bond prices can be communicated in two ways: (i) the price itself, which represents the sum of the present value of these cash flows; and (ii) the interest rate used to determine the price of the bond. The latter is often called a bond's yield to maturity (YTM) and is the interest rate implied by the payment structure.

Let T be the maturity of the bond and C(1), C(2) ... C(T) be the future cash flows; the yield to maturity is the rate of return which satisfies:

$$P = \frac{C(1)}{1+y} + \frac{C(2)}{(1+y)^2} + ... + \frac{C(T)}{(1+y)^T}$$

If the bond pays a constant coupon C and a final payment (the par value) of D at maturity, then the yield to maturity must now solve:

$$P = \frac{C}{1+y} + \frac{C}{(1+y)^2} + ... + \frac{C+D}{(1+y)^T}$$

Hopefully it is clear that there is an inverse relationship between the price of a security and its yield to maturity. If the yield to maturity increases, the market price of the bond will decrease.

Example

Consider a bond issued in November 2013 that pays an annual coupon of 1.25%, and expires in November 2017. If it has a par value of €1,000 and the yield to maturity is 1.5%, what is the price of this bond?

$$P = \frac{C(1)}{1+y} + \frac{C(2)}{(1+y)^2} + \frac{C(3)}{(1+y)^3} + \frac{C(4)}{(1+y)^4}$$

C(1) = C(2) = C(3) = 1.25% of €1,000 = 0.0125 x €1,000 = €12.50

C(4) = €12.50 + €1,000

y = 1.5% = 0.015

$$P = \frac{12.50}{1.015} + \frac{12.50}{1.015^2} + \frac{12.50}{1.015^3} + \frac{12.50+1000}{1.015^4}$$

P = 12.32 + 12.13 + 11.95 + 953.96 = €990.36

In November 2013, investors were willing to pay €930.36 for a bond issued by Tesco that paid €12.50 in November 2014, €12.50 in November 2015, €12.50 in November 2016 and €1012.50 in November 2017.

As the price is below the par value of €1,000, we say that the bond is priced at a discount.

Recall that a bond price is:

$$P = \frac{C}{1+y} + \frac{C}{(1+y)^2} + \ldots + \frac{C+D}{(1+y)^T}$$

This can also be considered as an annuity paying C with maturity T and one final payment of D at time T. If we use the notation, then let $a_{\overline{n}|i}$ denote the present value of the annuity, with a life of n at a rate of interest of i, paying 1 unit.

$a_{\overline{n}|i}$ can be found using $\left[\frac{1}{i} - \frac{1}{i(1+i)^n}\right]$ and the present value of the par value is, of course, simply $\frac{D}{(1+i)^n}$.

$$\left[\frac{1}{i} - \frac{1}{i(1+i)^n}\right] = \left[\frac{1}{0.015} - \frac{1}{i(1+0.015)^4}\right] = \left[66.667 - \frac{66.667}{1.0614}\right] = 3.8566$$

3.8566 x €12.50 = €48.21

$$\frac{D}{(1+i)^n} = \frac{1000}{(1+0.015)^4} \, 942.18.$$

€48.21 + €942.18 = €990.39 – the discrepancy is due to rounding errors.

Note Excel has a function, PV, to find the annuity value. Excel interprets the outcome as the cost to *you* of making these payments, so it is essential to insert a minus sign before the PV. i.e. = –PV(0.015,4,12.5), where 0.015 (or 1.5%) is the interest rate per period, 4 is the total number of periods in the annuity and 5 represents the payment per period. The answer is then 48.18.

The spreadsheet for this exercise can be found at https://www.liverpooluniversitypress.co.uk/pages/essentials-of-financial-management-efm. Please ensure you click on Section 4 and the 4.2 tab at the bottom of the spreadsheet.

4.3 The price yield curve

Consider a 30-year bond, with a face value of $1,000, paying a 10% coupon (i.e. $100) each year. The chart below shows the relationship between the price of the bond and the yield to maturity.

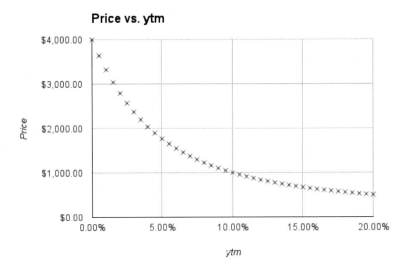

We can observe the following:

i. A negative relationship between price and yield to maturity (YTM), such that if the YTM on a bond rises, the price of the bond falls.

ii. A non-linear relationship between price and YTM. In particular as the YTM rises, price drops but at a lesser rate, i.e. as the YTM rises, the slope of the line becomes flatter.

iii. When the YTM equals the coupon of 10%, the bond price is equal to the par value of $1,000. If the YTM is below the coupon rate of 10%, the bond is priced at a premium to the par value of $1,000. If the YTM is greater than the coupon rate of 10%, the bond is priced at a discount to the par value of $1,000.

The spreadsheet for this exercise can be found at https://www.liverpooluniversitypress.co.uk/pages/essentials-of-financial-management-efm. Please ensure you click on Section 4 and the 4.3 tab at the bottom of the spreadsheet.

Note the price yield curve becomes more convex as maturity increases.

4.4 The risk of default

In March 2012, following the fallout from the global financial crisis, the YTM on a zero coupon bond issued by the German government, with a face value of €1,000, was 1.79% p.a. Meanwhile, the YTM on an identical Greek government bond was 38.97% p.a.

Using these two YTMs, what would the price of the two zero coupon bonds be?

$$P_{GERMANY} = \frac{€1000}{(1 + 0.0179)^{10}} = €837.43$$

$$P_{GREECE} = \frac{€1000}{(1 + 0.3897)^{10}} = €37.22$$

That is, the promise of receiving €1,000 from Germany was valued at €837.43, but the same promise, backed by the Greek government, was valued at just €37.22. Thus, to finance the same budget deficit, the Greek government would need to offer promises to repay over €22,000 compared to just €1,000 in Germany. The reason for this situation was the markets' view of the likelihood of default on the promise to repay by the Greek government, which was greater than the likelihood of default by the German government.

The likelihood of default is more commonly known as the risk of default and it is measured by a bond's rating. Moody's and Standard and Poor's are two well-known rating agencies. Rating agencies evaluate the ability of the bond issuer, whether a company or a government, to make future coupon and par payments. It follows that the "better" the rating, the lower the risk of default and subsequently the lower the yield that market participants will use to evaluate bond prices.

Since the primary function of bonds as an investment vehicle is to make fixed payments, it is essential that the company or government issuing the debt has the ability to make all payments on time and in full. Bond ratings evaluate the debt issuer to determine the risk of default.

The leading rating agencies assign ratings when a bond is first issued, and that rating helps determine how high the bond's interest rate will be. If the agencies assign a high rating, that means there is little risk of default, so the issuer can obtain a lower interest rate.

Standard and Poor's (S&P) assign a rating from AAA to D, and ratings from AA to CCC are modified by the addition of a plus or a minus. Bonds that are rated BBB and above are referred to as investment grade. Bonds that are rated below BBB are referred to as speculative grade. As of January 2013, the S&P rating of Greece, following the European sovereign debt crisis, was B–, whereas the S&P rating of Germany was AAA.

4.5. Does the yield to maturity change?

A common misconception is that as the payout from a bond is fixed, then the price is also fixed. This is not the case. As the market's perception of future risk changes, so does the price of the bond.

For example, consider a bond with an annual coupon of 8.625% p.a., expiring in eleven years, that is trading at par (i.e. £100). If in three years' time the bond is trading at £130, what must have happened to the yield on the bond? Given the negative relationship between bond prices and YTM, in order for the price of the bond to have risen the yield must have fallen. In fact, now with eight years to maturity, the YTM must have fallen to 4.1428%. As the YTM reflects the market's view on the ability of the bond issuer to make the coupon and final par payments, if it falls this will be as a result of the market viewing an improved capacity for the issuer to make such payments. Conversely, if the price of a bond falls it is due to the market having a diminished view of the ability of the issuer to make future coupon and par payments.

YTM	4.1428%	C = 8.625%	Par = £100
Year	CF	PV	
1	£8.625	£8.282	
2	£8.625	£7.952	
3	£8.625	£7.636	
4	£8.625	£7.332	
5	£8.625	£7.041	
6	£8.625	£6.761	
7	£8.625	£6.492	
8	£108.625	£78.505	
	Price = £130		

Of course, there are two conflicting forces when you discount the future cash flows of a bond – the passage of time and the market's perception of risk. Hence, the price could still fall, even if the perception of risk falls, as the bond gets closer to maturity. Moreoever, different bonds have different sensitivities to changes in interest rates, depending on their maturity and their coupon.

The spreadsheet for this exercise can be found at https://www.liverpooluniversitypress.co.uk/pages/essentials-of-financial-management-efm. Please ensure you click on Section 4 and the 4.5 tab at the bottom of the spreadsheet.

4.6 Bond duration

In section 2.6 we learned that beta measures the sensitivity of a stock to movements in the market. The equivalent concept for a bond is its duration. A bond's duration measures how sensitive the price of a bond is to a (small) change in yield to maturity.

Duration can be found as follows:

$$D = \frac{\sum_{t=1}^{T} \frac{tC_t}{(1+r)^t}}{P}$$

Expanding out the summation sign:

$$D = \frac{1 \times \frac{C_1}{(1+i)} + 2 \times \frac{C_2}{(1+i)^2} + ... + T \times \frac{C_T}{(1+i)^T}}{P}$$

The duration can therefore be calculated by computing the present value (PV) of the cash flows, and then multiplying them by the time indices.

The duration of a zero coupon bond is simply equal to its maturity. Returning to the equation above, and setting all coupon payments, prior to maturity, to zero, we can determine that:

$$D = \frac{T \times \frac{C_T}{(1+i)^T}}{P} = T$$

It follows that if a bond makes coupon payments prior to maturity then the duration of a coupon-paying bond is less than the term to maturity, T.

Example

Find the duration of a ten-year bond, with a face value of €1,000, paying annual coupon of 10%. Assume a YTM of 8%.

Par=	€1,000.00			
Coupon=	10.00%			
ytm=	8.00%			

Year	CF	PV	t x PV	
1	€100.00	€92.59	€92.59	
2	€100.00	€85.73	€171.47	
3	€100.00	€79.38	€238.15	
4	€100.00	€73.50	€294.01	
5	€100.00	€68.06	€340.29	
6	€100.00	€63.02	€378.10	
7	€100.00	€58.35	€408.44	
8	€100.00	€54.03	€432.22	
9	€100.00	€50.02	€450.22	
10	€1,100.00	€509.51	€5,095.13	
	Price=-	€1,134.20	7,900.63	<<=Sum of t x PV
	D=	6.97		

With regard to the following equation:

$$D = \frac{1 \times \dfrac{80}{(1+0.1)} + 2 \times \dfrac{80}{(1+0.1)^2} + ... + 10 \times \dfrac{1080}{(1+0.1)^{10}}}{P}$$

The price is the sum of the time period multiplied by the present value of the individual cash flows, which sums to 7,900.63. This is then divided by the price, which is the PV of the cash flows (CF) and equals €1,134.20 (at a premium to par, as the YTM is less than the coupon).

The duration is then:

7,900.63/1,134.20 = 6.97 years

The units for duration in this case are years, as in the numerator we are taking a time value, measured in years, and multiplying this by a euro amount. We then divide this by another euro amount. The euro amounts cancel and we are left with the units of years.

The column chart below depicts the annual cash flows alongside the associated present values.

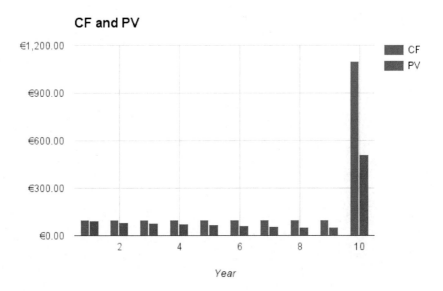

The actual maturity of this bond is ten years, but the duration or "effective" maturity of this bond is almost seven years.

Activity 4.1

Manually obtain the duration of a three-year bond, with a par of €1,000, an annual coupon of 5% and a YTM of 10%.

The spreadsheet for this exercise can be found at https://www.liverpool universitypress.co.uk/pages/essentials-of-financial-management-efm. Please ensure you click on Section 4 and the 4.6 tab at the bottom of the spreadsheet.

4.7 Characteristics of duration

The diagram below plots duration for four bonds:

- Bond 1 – zero coupon priced at a yield of 15%
- Bond 2 – 15% coupon priced at a yield of 6%.

- Bond 3 – 3% coupon priced at a yield of 15%
- Bond 4 – 15% coupon priced at a yield of 15%

Duration relationships

It follows that:

i.   **The duration of a coupon bond will always be less than its term to maturity** – note that bonds 2, 3 and 4 all have a duration less than that of bond 1.

ii. **An inverse relationship exists between coupon and duration** – a bond with a larger coupon will have a shorter duration as more of the total cash flows come earlier – bonds 3 and 4 are both priced at a yield of 15%, but bond 3 has a lower coupon than bond 4. At all maturities the duration of bond 3 is higher than the duration of bond 4.

iii. **A bond with no coupon payments will have a duration equal to its term to maturity** – see bond 1.

iv. **A positive relationship generally holds between term to maturity and duration, but duration increases at a decreasing rate with maturity** – note how the slope of bond 1 gets flatter as maturity increases.

v.   **There is an inverse relationship between yield to maturity and duration** – bonds 2 and 4 both have the same coupon but bond 2 is priced at a yield of 6%, whereas bond 4 is priced at a yield of 15%. At all maturities the duration of bond 4 is less than the duration of bond 2.

The spreadsheet for this exercise can be found at https://www.liverpooluniversitypress.co.uk/pages/essentials-of-financial-management-efm. Please ensure you click on Section 4 and the 4.7 tab at the bottom of the spreadsheet.

4.8 Relationship between bond prices and duration

Earlier it was observed that duration is to bonds as beta is to stocks. With regard to stocks, the greater the beta, the more a change in market return will impact on stock prices. Likewise with bonds, the greater the duration, the more a change in yield to maturity will impact on price. Note from section 4.3 that the relationship is a negative one, hence the greater the duration, the more an increase in yield to maturity will reduce bond prices.

It can be shown that:

$$\frac{\Delta P_0}{P_0} = -D\frac{\Delta(1+i)}{(1+i)}$$

It is often convenient to divide duration by $(1 + i)$ and call the result modified duration:

$$D_m = \frac{D}{1+i}$$

It follows then that:

$$\frac{\Delta P_0}{P_0} = -D\frac{\Delta(1+i)}{(1+i)} =$$

$$-D_m \times (1+i) \times \frac{\Delta(1+i)}{(1+i)} = -D_m \times \Delta(1+i)$$

$$\frac{\Delta P_0}{P_0} = -D_m \times \Delta(1+i)$$

Hence the proportionate change in bond prices is negatively and linearly related to changes in yield to maturity.

Example

Earlier, in section 4.6, we found the duration of a ten-year bond, with a face value of €1,000, paying annual coupon of 10% and assuming a YTM of 8%, to be 6.97 years. The price was €1,134.20.

According to the relationship outlined above, what does duration predict the new bond price will be if the YTM changes to (i) 8.1%, (ii) 8.5%, (iii) 9%?

$D = 6.97, D_m = 6.97/1.08 = 6.45$

(i) $\dfrac{\Delta P_0}{P_0} = -D_m \times \Delta(1 + i) = -6.45 \times 0.001 = -0.645\%$

new price = €1,134.20 x (1 + (-0.00645)) = €1,126.88

(ii)   8.5

new price = €1,134.20 x (1 + (-0.03225)) = €1,097.62

(iii) $\dfrac{\Delta P_0}{P_0} = -D_m \times \Delta(1 + i) = -6.45 \times 0.01 = -6.45\%$

new price = €1,134.20 x (1 + (-0.0645)) = €1,061.94.

Frederick Macaulay first proposed the measure of duration to represent the average maturity of a stream of payments in *Some Theoretical Problems suggested by the Movements of Interest Rates, Bond Yields, and Stock Prices in the United States since 1856.*[1] As this was many years before the invention of the spreadsheet or the calculator, the ability to estimate a bond's price using just the duration and the change in interest rates was particularly attractive. Nowadays it would be a trivial exercise to find the new bond price, given the new interest rate.

With regard to the three scenarios above, the actual prices, i.e. if we repriced, are presented below.

Change	Estimated price	Actual price	Error
+0.1%	€1,126.88	€1,126.92	€0.04
+0.5%	€1,097.62	€1,098.42	€0.8
+1.0%	€1,061.94	€1,064.18	€2.24

---

[1] Frederick Macaulay, *Some Theoretical Problems suggested by the Movements of Interest Rates, Bond Yields, and Stock Prices in the United States since 1856* (New York: Columbia University Press for the National Bureau of Economic Research, 1938).

Note that in each case the estimate of the new bond price, using duration, is less than the actual price. That is, we underestimate the bond price when yields rise. Note further that the extent of the underestimation varies with the size of the change of interest rates. When the change was 0.1%, the error was just 4 cents, but when the change was 1% the error was €2.24.

This relationship is depicted in the diagram below. The tangent drawn on the price yield curve represents duration and when we use the relationship:

$$\frac{\Delta P_0}{P_0} = -D_m \times \Delta(1+i)$$

we are assuming a linear relationship between bond price changes and yield changes, when in fact the relationship is convex. It is evident from the diagram that the larger the change in yield, the greater the error.

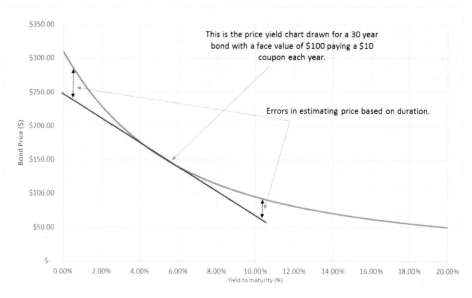

This is the price yield chart drawn for a 30 year bond with a face value of $100 paying a $10 coupon each year.

Errors in estimating price based on duration.

The spreadsheet for this exercise can be found at https://www.liverpooluniversitypress.co.uk/pages/essentials-of-financial-management-efm. Please ensure you click on Section 4 and the 4.8 tab at the bottom of the spreadsheet.

4.9 Bond convexity

In order to correct for the error in estimating the change in bond price, due to the convex nature between price and yield to maturity, we must add in the following term:

$$C \left[\frac{\Delta(1+i)}{(1+i)} \right]^2$$

where:

$$C = \frac{1}{2} \frac{\sum_{t=1}^{T} \frac{t(t+1)C_t}{(1+i)^t}}{P}$$

The calculation of convexity is very similar to that of duration with an additional step of multiplying the time step by the present value of cash flows by a further (1 + time step). Returning to the earlier example:

Par=	€1,000.00				
Coupon=	10.00%				
ytm=	8.00%				
Year	CF	PV	t x PV	t x (t+1) x PV	
1	€100.00	€92.59	€92.59	€185.19	
2	€100.00	€85.73	€171.47	€514.40	
3	€100.00	€79.38	€238.15	€952.60	
4	€100.00	€73.50	€294.01	€1,470.06	
5	€100.00	€68.06	€340.29	€2,041.75	
6	€100.00	€63.02	€378.10	€2,646.71	
7	€100.00	€58.35	€408.44	€3,267.55	
8	€100.00	€54.03	€432.22	€3,889.94	
9	€100.00	€50.02	€450.22	€4,502.24	
10	€1,100.00	€509.51	€5,095.13	€56,046.41	
	Price=-	€1,134.20	7,900.63	75,516.84	<<Sum of t x (t+1) x PV
	D=	6.97			
	C=	33.29			

The sum of the t x (t + 1) x PV is 75,516.84. If we multiply this by 0.5 and divide by the price of €1,134.20 we arrive at a figure for convexity of 33.29.

The spreadsheet for this exercise can be found at https://www.liverpooluniversitypress.co.uk/pages/essentials-of-financial-management-efm. Please ensure you click on Section 4 and the 4.9 tab at the bottom of the spreadsheet.

You can vary the coupon and duration to note the impact on duration and convexity.

Returning to the example above, we had predicted a fall in price, just using duration, of 6.45% when yields rose by 1%. The additional correction from convexity would be:

$$33.29 \times (0.01/1.08)^2 = 0.285\%$$

The total change would then be:

$$-6.45\% + 0.285\% = -6.165\%$$

If the price were €1,134.20, then the estimated price would be:

$$€1,134.20 \times (1 + (-0.06165)) = €1,064.28$$

This compares to an actual price of €1,064.18, hence the error in estimation is much smaller.

5
Investment appraisal

5.1 Introduction to investment appraisal

In this chapter we will evaluate real investment decisions whereby entrepreneurs and companies consider whether a certain level of investment will generate sufficient cash flows in the future to make the investment worthwhile. In this section you will be introduced to three main forms of investment appraisal: (i) payback, (ii) net present value (NPV) and (iii) internal rate of return (IRR). We will also look at combinations of these.

Graham and Harvey[1] surveyed 392 chief financial officers (CFOs) and asked them a variety of questions about capital budgeting decisions. They found that "Most respondents select net present value and internal rate of return as their most frequently used capital budgeting techniques; 74.9% of CFOs always or almost always ... use net present value ... and 75.7% always or almost always use internal rate of return ..."

When asked to state, on a scale of 0 (never) to 4 (always), "how frequently does your firm use the following techniques when deciding which projects or acquisitions to pursue?", the mean score was 3.09 for IRR, 3.08 for NPV and 2.53 for payback for the entire sample of firms.

---

[1] John R. Graham and Campbell R. Harvey, 'The theory and practice of corporate finance: evidence from the field', *Journal of Financial Economics*, 60.2–3 (2001), pp. 187–243, https://doi.org/10.1016/S0304-405X(01)00044-7

However, for small firms the mean score was 2.87, 2.83 and 2.72 respectively, while for large firms it was 3.41, 3.42 and 2.25 respectively. It is evident that payback is preferred by small firms but NPV and IRR is more popular with large firms.

5.2 The net present value decision rule

We have previously seen that a dollar today is worth more than a dollar in the future. It is therefore not appropriate to focus on the actual level of future cash flows, as in "present value" terms they will decline over time. Therefore, if we wish to evaluate an investment project we need to focus on discounted cash flows, not the actual level of cash flows.

Moreover, previously we have learned that equities and bonds carry with them different degrees of risk and hence have different required rates of return. It follows that the interest rate used to discount cash flows will vary from investment to investment.

The net present value of a project can be found by:

$$NPV = -I_0 + \sum_{t=1}^{T} \frac{CF_t}{(1+r)^t}$$

where I_0 represents the initial investment in time period 0, CF_t represents the cash flow in period t, r is the required rate of return and T is the time of the final cash flow. Note that CF_t can be positive or negative. The nature of the cash flows that are considered in net present value evaluation are referred to as incremental cash flows, i.e. cash flows that are added to a firm's existing cash flows as a result of accepting the project. In addition the project should consider any external effects that the project would have. For example, cannibalisation is an externality in which the investment reduces cash flows elsewhere in the company; for example, the launch of a new product may take sales away from existing products.

Often when a project is being considered there would have been prior spending such as marketing consultancy or a feasibility study. These costs are referred to as sunk costs and would be incurred whether the project was accepted or not. As such, these costs would not affect the future cash flows and should not be considered.

Example

Consider three investment projects, A, B and C, whose incremental cash flows are detailed below. The sum of the three projects' incremental cash flows are identical at $1.2m; however the three projects differ in their timing, and as we have seen in section 5.1, the timing of the cash flows influences the discount factor, which in turn influences the present values.

Without doing any calculations, what would the ranking of the projects be?

Project/Year	0	1	2	3	4
A	−$2m	$1.6m	$1.6m		
B	−$2m			$1.6m	$1.6m
C	−$1m	$1.6m	$0.6m		

As a dollar in the future is worth less than a dollar today, we will clearly prefer projects that deliver cash in earlier periods. In this case we would favour projects A and C over project B. It follows that we would also prefer projects that require less initial investment; hence we would prefer project C over project A. The ranking is therefore: C then A then B.

The NPV decision rule is as follows:

> accept any project if its NPV > 0 or if NPV = 0
>
> reject a project if its NPV < 0

The notion that a project with a small, or even zero, NPV should be accepted often causes bewilderment. The rationale is that as long as the project is evaluated at a discount rate commensurate with its risk, then the providers of capital (bondholders and shareholders) are receiving their expected return and hence the project should be accepted.

A very simple model of company valuation proposes a company's value as:

> value of net assets + present value of future opportunities

Hence if we accept a project, albeit with a very small NPV, then we are still increasing the value of the company.

Example

Assume the cash flows from the construction and sale of student accommodation are as follows:

Year 0	Year 1	Year 2
−$300,000	−$200,000	+$600,000

Assuming a 7% required rate of return, using the NPV decision rule would this project be accepted?

If r = 7% = 0.07, then the three discount factors are:

> Year 0: 1/1.07 = 1

Year 1: $1/1.07^2 = 0.935$

Year 2: $1/1.07^3 = 0.873$

The NPV is then:

$-\$300,000 + 0.935 \times -\$200,000 + 0.873 \times \$600,000 = \$36,800$

On the basis of NPV we should therefore accept this project.

Note that the above answer assumes rounding to three decimal places. The actual answer, with no rounding, is $37,147.35.

In section 4.1 you were introduced to the Excel function PV, which is able to find the present value of a future stream of equal cash flows. It is not appropriate to use that function here and instead we must use the NPV function. For example:

=npv(0.07,-200000,600000)

This returns the result $337,145.35, which represents the present value (at 7%) of cash flows of −$200,000 and $600,000 in years 1 and 2 respectively. If we deduct from this the initial investment of $300,000, we arrive at the previous answer of $37,145.35

Suppose you own a food van at a football stadium that sells pies, chips, burgers, soft drinks and hot drinks. You have five years left on your contract and do not expect it to be renewed. Your busiest period is the 15-minute half-time break, and long queues limit your sales. You have developed three different proposals to reduce the queues and increase profits. The table below shows the incremental cash flows.

Project/Year	0	1	2	3	4	5
Reconfigure van to serve from both sides	-$75,000	$40,000	$40,000	$40,000	$40,000	$40,000
Install more efficient equipment	-$25,000	$20,000	$20,000	$20,000	$20,000	$20,000
Buy a bigger van	-$150,000	$60,000	$60,000	$60,000	$60,000	$60,000

You have decided that a 15% discount rate is appropriate, given the risk of the investment. What is the NPV of each proposal?

Project/Year	NPV
Reconfigure van to serve from both sides	$59,086.20
Install more efficient equipment	$42,043.10
Buy a bigger van	$51,129.31

Clearly the owner of the hot food van can only choose one of the outcomes. The projects are therefore considered to be mutually exclusive. On the basis of the NPV calculations above, the best decision is to reconfigure the van so that it can serve from both sides.

The spreadsheet for this exercise can be found at https://www.liverpooluniversitypress.co.uk/pages/essentials-of-financial-management-efm. Please ensure you click on Section 5 and the 5.2 tab at the bottom of the spreadsheet.

5.3 The relationship between NPV and discount rate

Consider once again the equation for the present value of a cash flow:

$$PV = \frac{1}{(1+r)^t} \times Cash\ Flow$$

The first term above is the discount factor. Hopefully it is evident that the larger is r, then the larger the denominator and the smaller is the discount factor. Returning once again to the example in section 5.2:

Year 0	Year 1	Year 2
−$300,000	−$200,000	+$600,000

As r increases, the present value of the positive cash flow will decrease. At the same time the PV of the second construction payment in year 1 will also decrease, though that will be viewed as an advantage from the investor's point of view.

Using the NPV function in Excel it is trivial to plot NPV against the discount rate.

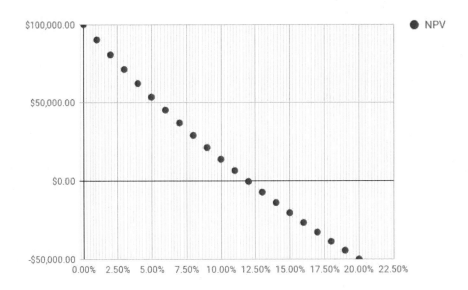

From the chart above it is evident that there is a negative and non-linear relationship between NPV and discount rates. It is also evident that eventually, as r increases, there is some discount rate whereby the sum of the present values of future incremental cash flows exactly offsets the cash flow in year 0 and the net present value is zero. In the chart above this appears to happen at a discount rate of approximately 12%. Note that this diagram is near identical to the diagram in Chapter 4 depicting the relationship between bond prices and yield to maturity, albeit here we have a cash flow out in year 0 which causes the curve to shift downwards.

Revisiting a previous example:

Project/Year	0	1	2	3	4
A	–$2m	$1.6m	$1.6m		
B	–$2m			$1.6m	$1.6m
C	–$1m	$1.6m	$0.6m		

At a discount rate of zero all three projects have an NPV of zero, but when depicted graphically it is clear that, due to the latter's cash flows, project B's NPV becomes zero much sooner than that of the other two projects.

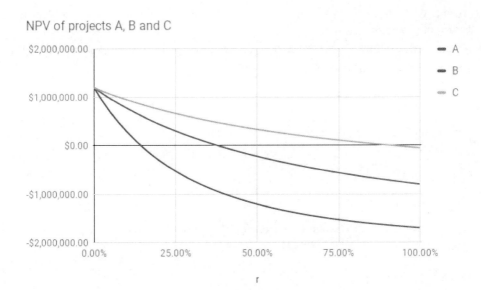

NPV of projects A, B and C

The spreadsheet for this exercise can be found at https://www.liverpooluniversitypress.co.uk/pages/essentials-of-financial-management-efm. Please ensure you click on Section 5 and the 5.3 tab at the bottom of the spreadsheet.

5.4 The internal rate of return

It is evident in the example above that there is some r for which the NPV of a project is zero. This r is referred to as the internal rate of return (IRR). The formal definition of a project's IRR is the rate of discount which, when applied to the project's cash flows, produces a zero NPV.

The IRR decision rule is then:

> invest in any project that has an IRR greater than or equal to some predetermined cost of capital

The comparison rate is usually the cost of capital, i.e. the discount rate we would have used in an NPV analysis. This is often referred to as the hurdle rate, which makes logical sense, as r reflects the riskiness of the project and, as the risk of the project increases, a higher IRR is required to overcome the higher hurdle. The three projects, A, B and C, analysed earlier have "standard" cash flows, i.e. up-front investment followed by cash inflows. For projects with "standard" cash flows the relationship between NPV and r will be a negative one as depicted in section 5.3 above.

When the length of the project is two periods or less it is a trivial exercise to find the IRR. In particular, returning to project C above, we are solving:

$$-1 + \frac{1.6}{1+r} + \frac{0.6}{(1+r)^2} = 0$$

Multiplying through by $(1 + r)^2$:

$$-1(1+r)^2 + 1.6(1+r) + 0.6 = 0$$

Setting $(1 + r) = x$:

$$-x^2 + 1.6x + 0.6 = 0$$

which many students will recognise as a quadratic equation in the form:

$$ax^2 + bx + c = 0$$

Hence, a = –1, b = 1.6 and c = 0.6.

The solution to a quadratic equation can be found as:

$$x = \frac{-b \pm \sqrt{b^2 - 4ac}}{2a}$$

$$x = \frac{-1.6 \pm \sqrt{1.6 - 4 \times (-1) \times 0.6}}{2 \times (-1)}$$

x = –0.3136 or 1.9136

As x = 1 + r, then r = x – 1. We can therefore discard the solution –0.3136 and instead use the other solution. Therefore the r that solves the above equation is 0.9136 or 91.36%. Note that here the answer is independent of the amounts. For example, we would have found the answer to be 91.36% regardless of whether the cash flows were –1m, 1.6m, 0.6m or –2m, 3.2m, 1.2m or –1bn, 1.6bn, 0.6bn. Check this for yourself.

Excel has a built-in IRR function. For example, if you enter "=IRR({-1,1.6,0.6})" in Excel you will obtain the answer of 91.36%.

Using the IRR function in Excel gives the internal rates of return to be 38% (project A), 14.4% (project B) and 91.4% (project C), which corresponds with the order in the diagram in section 5.3.

The spreadsheet for this exercise can be found at https://www.liverpooluniversitypress.co.uk/pages/essentials-of-financial-management-efm. Please ensure you click on Section 5 and the 5.4a tab at the bottom of the spreadsheet.

It is also possible to find the IRR of any project manually. Returning to the previous example of the hot food van, buying a bigger van required a cash investment, in year 0, of $150,000. This was followed by positive cash flows of $60,000 for the next five years.

If we have an initial estimate of the NPV at 20%, we find it to be $29,436.73. If we had returned a negative value, we would then have tried a lower discount rate until we returned a positive answer. Now we re-estimate the NPV at a higher discount rate, say 30%, and find the NPV to be −$3,865.81.

We can then find the IRR via interpolation.

$i_0 = 0.2$, $i_1 = 0.3$, $NPV_0 = 29,436.73$, $NPV_1 = -3,865.81$.

Inserting these values into the equation below:

$$IRR = i_0 + (i_1 - i_0) \times \frac{NPV_0}{NPV_0 + |NPV_1|}$$

$$IRR = 0.2 + (0.3 - 0.2) \times \frac{29,436.73}{29,436.73 + |-3,865.81|} = 28.84\%$$

Note the pair of vertical lines indicates the absolute value.

The actual value for IRR, found using the IRR function, was 28.65%. The relationship between NPV and r, for values of r from 20% to 30%, is depicted below. Essentially, the equation above defines a chord between the coordinates (20%, $29,436.73) and (30%, −$3,865.81) and determines where that chord intersects the horizontal axis.

NPV vs. r

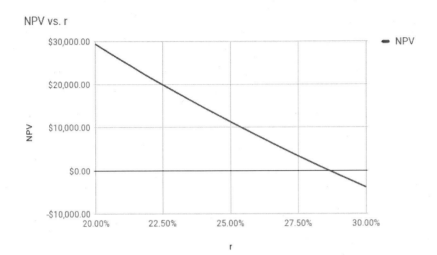

Example

A bespoke kitchen-maker can purchase a specialist machine for $40,000. The investment is expected to generate $20,000 and $40,000 in cash flows for two years respectively. Using the interpolation method outlined above, what is the IRR on this investment? If the kitchen-maker views the risk of the project to be commensurate with a discount rate of 20%, would you accept this project? Hint: use 25% as the initial guess and 35% as the higher guess.

i0	0.25		
Year	**0**	**1**	**2**
CF	−$40,000	$20,000	$40,000
PV	−$40,000	$16,000	$25,600
NPV0	**$1,600.00**		
i1	0.35		
Year	**0**	**1**	**2**
CF	−$40,000	$20,000	$40,000
PV	−$40,000	$14,814.81	$21,947.87
NPV1	**−$3,237.31**		
IRR	**28.31%**		

Note the "actual" IRR is 28.08%. If the hurdle rate is 20%, then on the basis of IRR this project should be accepted.

The spreadsheet for this exercise can be found at https://www.liverpooluniversitypress.co.uk/pages/essentials-of-financial-management-efm. Please ensure you click on Section 5 and the 5.4b tab at the bottom of the spreadsheet.

You can change the initial guesses in the spreadsheet above and observe the impact on the interpolated IRR. You should observe that the further apart the guesses are, the less accurate is the IRR.

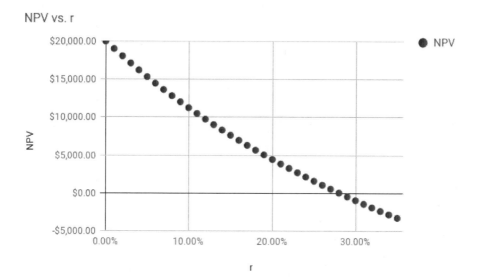

5.5 Pitfalls with using the internal rate of return

Certain cash flows can generate an NPV equal to zero at two different discount rates. Consider a project with the following cash flows:

Year	0	1	2	3	4
Cash flow	−$1,000,000	$800,000	$1,000,000	$1,300,000	−$2,200,000

The relationship between NPV and the discount rate is depicted below.

NPV vs. r

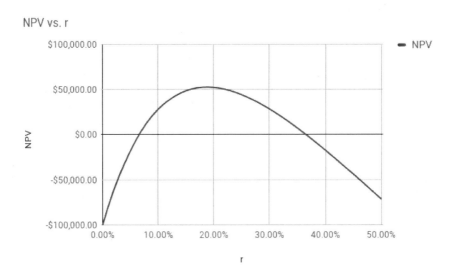

For this project there exist two IRRs: one at approximately 6.6% and another at approximately 36.6%, making it impossible to apply the IRR decision rule.

Traditional projects that require an initial investment followed by several years of positive cash flows generate a negative relationship between NPV and the discount rate. However, projects where the cash flows switch from positive to negative (and perhaps back again) produce a perverse relationship between NPV and the discount rate.

Consider a project with the following cash flows:

Year	0	1	2	3
Cash flow	$20,000	−$72,000	$86,400	−$34,560

The relationship between NPV and the discount rate is depicted below.

NPV vs. r

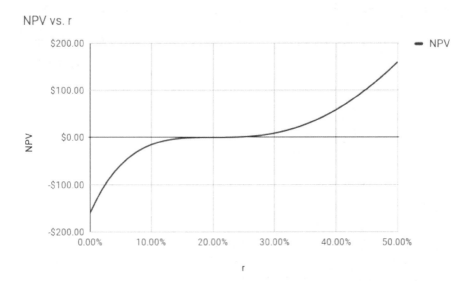

The IRR of this project is 20%.

This relationship is contrary to what we would normally expect. We would think that, since this project has an IRR of 20%, we should accept it. But if the opportunity cost of capital is 10%, less than the IRR, the project has a very small negative NPV and we should reject it.

The greatest weakness of the internal rate of return rule is its inability to handle mutually exclusive projects. When we have mutually exclusive projects, only one can be selected. This is in contrast to non-mutually exclusive projects where all those with a positive NPV should be accepted, since by doing so the value of the firm is increased. Examples of mutually exclusive projects include sole use of a scarce resource such as retail space or requiring one production technique to produce a product.

Example

Suppose that the Davenport Corporation has two alternative uses for a very large warehouse. It can store classic cars (investment A) or touring caravans (investment B). The cash flows are as follows:

Year	0	1	2	3
Cash flow (A)	−$200,000	$200,000	$20,000	$20,000
Cash flow (B)	−$200,000	$20,000	$20,000	$240,000

The chart below illustrates the NPV of these two projects at various discount rates.

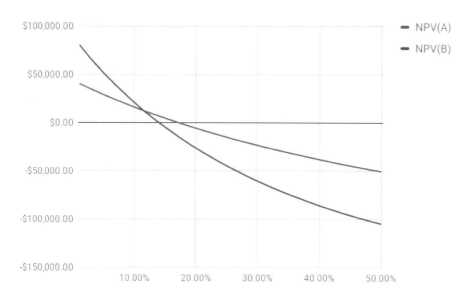

Both projects require the same up-front investment. However, project B's large cash flow occurs in period 3, whereas project A's large cash flow occurs in period 1. Consequently, at lower discount rates the benefit from the extra net cash flow of $40,000 from project B makes it the preferred project. But as the discount rate rises, and the $240,000 period 3 cash flow is discounted more heavily, project A becomes the preferred project. The investment decision, at various discount rates, is detailed below:

Discount rate	NPV(A)	NPV(B)	Decision
5%	$25,893.53	$44,509.23	Accept Project B
10%	$13,373.40	$15,026.30	Accept Project B
15%	$2,186.24	−$9,681.93	Accept Project A
20%	−$7,870.37	−$30,555.56	Accept neither

Using the NPV decision rule it is therefore clear that the decision depends on the adopted discount rate. There is one discount rate, 10.55%, where investors are indifferent between the two projects. This is referred to as the crossover rate and how to calculate it is detailed in section 5.6.

Due to the pattern of the cash flows, the NPV of project B tends towards zero faster than that of project A, and the two IRRs are 16.04% and 12.94% for projects A and B respectively. If we assume a hurdle rate of, for example, 10%, it is tempting when using the IRR rule to select project A, as the margin that the IRR has over the hurdle rate is larger. However, at a discount rate of 10%, the NPV rule would select project B. Therefore, in the face of mutually exclusive projects, the IRR rule is unable to distinguish between them.

The spreadsheet for this exercise can be found at https://www.liverpooluniversitypress.co.uk/pages/essentials-of-financial-management-efm. Please ensure you click on Section 5 and the 5.5a, 5.5b and 5.5c tabs at the bottom of the spreadsheet.

5.6 The crossover rate

The crossover rate is the discount rate at which the NPVs of two projects are equal.

Assume that the first project requires an investment of A and its cash flows at the end of years 1, 2 and 3 are $CF_{A,1}$, $CF_{A,2}$ and $CF_{A,3}$; then the NPV is:

$$NPV_A = I_A + \frac{CF_{A,1}}{(1+r)^1} + \frac{CF_{A,2}}{(1+r)^2} + \frac{CF_{A,3}}{(1+r)^3}$$

If a second project requires an investment of B and generates cash flows of $CF_{B,1}$, $CF_{B,2}$ and $CF_{B,3}$, then the NPV is:

$$NPV_B = I_B + \frac{CF_{B,1}}{(1+r)^1} + \frac{CF_{B,2}}{(1+r)^2} + \frac{CF_{B,3}}{(1+r)^3}$$

At the crossover rate the NPVs of the two projects are equal; hence we can find it by equating the NPV for the first project with the NPV for the second project and solving for r:

$$I_A + \frac{CF_{A,1}}{(1+r)^1} + \frac{CF_{A,2}}{(1+r)^2} + \frac{CF_{A,3}}{(1+r)^3} = I_B + \frac{CF_{B,1}}{(1+r)^1} + \frac{CF_{B,2}}{(1+r)^2} + \frac{CF_{B,3}}{(1+r)^3}$$

Example

Returning to the cash flows in the Davenport Corporation example:

Year	0	1	2	3
Cash flow (A)	−$200,000	$200,000	$20,000	$20,000
Cash flow (B)	−$200,000	$20,000	$20,000	$240,000

If we want to solve this manually, we must combine both sets of cash flows into one problem, set the answer to zero and solve as in an IRR exercise:

$$I_A + \frac{CF_{A,1}}{(1+r)^1} + \frac{CF_{A,2}}{(1+r)^2} + \frac{CF_{A,3}}{(1+r)^3} = I_B + \frac{CF_{B,1}}{(1+r)^1} + \frac{CF_{B,2}}{(1+r)^2} + \frac{CF_{B,3}}{(1+r)^3}$$

Set this to zero by subtracting the NPV of project B from the NPV of project A:

$$I_A - I_B + \frac{CF_{A,1}}{(1+r)^1} + \frac{CF_{A,2}}{(1+r)^2} + \frac{CF_{A,3}}{(1+r)^3} - \frac{CF_{B,1}}{(1+r)^1} - \frac{CF_{B,2}}{(1+r)^2}$$
$$- \frac{CF_{B,3}}{(1+r)^3} = 0$$

$$I_A - I_B + \frac{\left(CF_{A,1} - CF_{B,1}\right)}{(1+r)^1} + \frac{\left(CF_{A,2} - CF_{B,2}\right)}{(1+r)^2} + \frac{\left(CF_{A,3} - CF_{B,3}\right)}{(1+r)^3} = 0$$

$$200{,}000 - 200{,}0000 + \frac{(200{,}000 - 20{,}000)}{(1+r)^1} + \frac{(20{,}000 - 20{,}000)}{(1+r)^2}$$
$$+ \frac{(20{,}000 - 240{,}000)}{(1+r)^3} = 0$$

$$\frac{180{,}000}{(1+r)^1} + \frac{0}{(1+r)^2} + \frac{-220{,}000}{(1+r)^3} = 0$$

$$\frac{180{,}000}{(1+r)^1} - \frac{220{,}000}{(1+r)^3} = 0$$

$$\frac{180{,}000}{(1+r)^1} = \frac{220{,}000}{(1+r)^3}$$

$$\frac{180{,}000}{1} = \frac{220{,}000}{(1+r)^2}$$

$$(1+r)^2 = \frac{220{,}000}{180{,}000}$$

$$r = \sqrt{\frac{220{,}000}{180{,}000}} - 1 = 10.55\%$$

The chart below confirms this result. It is clear that when the line representing the NPV of project A intersects with the line representing the NPV of project B, then the "NPVA-NPVB" line is zero.

NPV_A, NPV_B and NPVA-NPBV

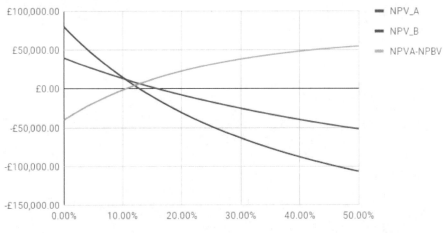

As both projects require the same investment, the project (A-B) can be considered as having non-standard cash flows of +$180,000 in year 1 and –$220,000 in year 3. If we switch the problem around and look at NPV of A – NPV of B, then the problem looks more familiar:

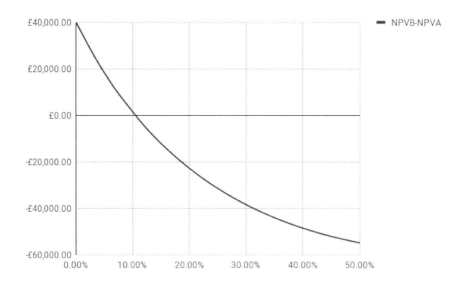

As a rule it is easier to evaluate the projects at a discount rate of zero and subtract the smaller NPV from the larger. At a discount rate of 0% the NPV of project B is $80,000, while the NPV of project A is $40,000. It is then a trivial exercise to find the IRR via interpolation:

$$IRR = i_0 + (i_1 - i_0) \times \frac{NPV_0}{NPV_0 + |NPV_1|}$$

NPV of B-A at 5% = $18,615.70, NPV of B-A at 15% = –$11,868.17

IRR = 0.05 + (0.15 – 0.05) x [[18,615.70]/[18,615.79 + |–11.868.17|]] = 11.1%

The actual answer is 10.55%, and we would get closer to that if we chose guesses closer together. Project B is preferred when the discount rate is less than 10.55%, but when the discount rate rises to over 10.55% project A is preferred.

The spreadsheet for this exercise can be found at https://www.liverpooluniversitypress.co.uk/pages/essentials-of-financial-management-efm. Please ensure you click on Section 5 and the 5.6 tab at the bottom of the spreadsheet.

5.7 Payback

After net present value (NPV) and internal rate of return (IRR), the next most popular form of investment appraisal is payback. According to Graham and Harvey, 56.74% of respondents always or almost always stated that they used the payback approach.[2]

Payback is extremely simple, as it merely calculates the time period taken to return the initial investment. It is often quoted in years and months or years and fractions of a year. For example, if a project requires an initial investment of $45,000 and returns cash flows of $15,000 per annum for five years, it is evident that this project returns the investment in three years. The payback period of three years would then be compared to the company's internally determined payback period, and if the project returns the investment within this payback period it will be accepted; if it doesn't, it will be rejected.

It is convention to assume that cash flows are evenly distributed throughout the time period. For example, revisiting the previous project, if the cash flows were $20,000 per annum then the payback period would be 2.25 years, as after year 2 $5,000 is outstanding and with a cash flow of $20,000 in year 3 this would arrive 0.25 of the way through the year.

A clear advantage of payback is that it is easy to understand and calculate. It is often used as a supplementary screening technique, especially in the case of mutually exclusive projects where IRR is unable to select the most appropriate. An obvious disadvantage of the payback approach is that it ignores the time value of money and ignores cash flows beyond the company's payback period. To overcome the issue of ignoring the time value of money it is possible to use modified payback, whereby we determine the number of periods required not to recover the actual level of cash flows, but the present value of cash flows.

Activity 5.1

Calculate the simple payback of a project that requires investment of $60,000 followed by annual cash flows of $25,000 for three years. Assuming a discount rate of 5% per annum, then calculate the modified payback.

---

[2] Graham and Harvey, 'The theory and practice of corporate finance', pp. 187–243.

6
The weighted average cost of capital

6.1 Determining the appropriate cost of capital

When undertaking NPV analysis it is important to use an appropriate discount rate, that is, to choose an interest rate that is commensurate with the risk of a project. Choosing an inappropriate discount rate can lead to the acceptance of a project that should have been rejected (or conversely the rejection of a project that should have been accepted).

In the survey by Graham and Harvey cited in section 5.7, 73.49% of respondents used the capital asset pricing model (CAPM) to determine the estimate the cost of capital.

Algebraically the CAPM can be expressed as:

$$E(R_i) = R_f + \beta[E(R_m) - R_f]$$

which in words means that the expected return on an asset (or portfolio) is equal to the risk-free rate (R_f) plus the asset (or portfolio) beta multiplied by the market risk premium [E(Rm) – R_f].

Credit Suisse produce an annual report entitled "Credit Suisse Global Investment Returns Yearbook". The 2017 edition is in the public domain.[1] Page 45 of this report details the risk premium, [E(Rm) – Rf], for the United Kingdom over the period 1900–2016 and finds it to be 4.4%. Over the more recent period of 1967–2016, equities have beaten Treasury bills by 5.1%.

Richard Roll and Steven Ross challenged William Sharpe's CAPM.[2] In their opinion, market risk is not the only risk that systematically affects all assets. They argued that factors such as interest rates, inflation, the position in the business cycle, and expectations about future economic performance all systematically affect assets. Moreover, just like the CAPM where assets were affected in different ways relative to the stock market, assets would have different sensitivities to these additional systematic factors. Sharpe's defence was that the stock market reflects all of these other factors. Roll and Ross's model is known as the arbitrage pricing theory (APT).

The APT states that the following risk–return relationship will result for security i.

$$E(R_i) = R_F + \beta_{i,F1}[E(R_{F1}) - R_F] + \beta_{i,F2}[E(R_{F2}) - R_F] + \ldots + \beta_{i,FH}[E(R_{FH}) - R_F]$$

where:

$\beta_{i,Fj}$ = the sensitivity of security i to the j'th factor.

$[E(R_{Fj}) - R_F]$ = the excess return of the j'th systematic factor over the risk free rate – this can be thought of as the price for the j'th systematic risk.

In section 2.7 we introduced the CAPM and the security market line (SML). $E(R_i) = R_f + \beta_i$ The SML states that investors are only compensated for holding market risk. The APT, by contrast, states that there are other systematic risks than market risk and that investors should be compensated for holding all types of systematic risk. However, the CAPM and APT are in agreement that investors are not compensated for holding unique risk.

Despite the clear advantages that the APT offers, the CAPM remains the most popular due to its ease of use. In order to implement the CAPM all you need is the beta, the market-risk premium and the risk-free rate. However, there is no consensus of opinion on the factors required for the APT.

---

[1] https://publications.credit-suisse.com/tasks/render/file/?fileID=B8FDD84D-A4CD-D983-12840F52F61BA0B4

[2] Richard Roll and Stephen A. Ross, 'An empirical investigation of the Arbitrage Pricing Theory', *Journal of Finance*, 35 (1980), pp. 1073–103.

Example

Betas are freely available on many finance websites. At the time of writing, the betas of Sky plc and Tesco plc were 1.34 and 0.29 respectively. If a company was appraising a project with the same risks as are inherent in a company like Sky or Tesco, then the required returns could be found to be:

> Treasury bill rate = 0.21%
>
> market-risk premium = 4.4%
>
> Tesco: E(R) = 0.21 + 0.29 x 4.4 = 1.486%
>
> Sky: E(R) = 0.21 + 1.34 x 4.4 = 6.106%

It is evident that the risk inherent in a supermarket chain such as Tesco is less than that inherent in a subscription-based service such as Sky. Consequently, the returns demanded by investors in Sky are significantly higher than those of Tesco. Likewise, when appraising future cash flows from investment projects, the cash flows are discounted more heavily for Sky than Tesco.

6.2 The cost of debt capital

The term "cost of debt" is interchangeable with the yield to maturity on a bond. Essentially this is the interest rate that equates the present value of the stream of future coupon payments and the payment of the par value to the current market price. The good thing from a company's point of view is that interest payments are tax-deductible, i.e. at a 23% corporation tax rate for every £1 of interest paid, the company's tax liability falls by 23p.

Therefore $K_{dat} = K_d(1 - T_c)$

Example

Consider a bond that expires in 20 years' time, with a par value of £100, paying annual coupons of 6.15%. If the current market price is £97.5, what is the cost of debt? Assuming a corporate tax rate of 23%, what is the cost of debt after tax?

kd	6.375%
Par	£100
Coupon	6.15%

Year	CF	PV
1	£6.15	£5.78
2	£6.15	£5.43
3	£6.15	£5.11
4	£6.15	£4.80
5	£6.15	£4.52
6	£6.15	£4.24
7	£6.15	£3.99
8	£6.15	£3.75
9	£6.15	£3.53
10	£6.15	£3.31
11	£6.15	£3.12
12	£6.15	£2.93
13	£6.15	£2.75
14	£6.15	£2.59
15	£6.15	£2.43
16	£6.15	£2.29
17	£6.15	£2.15
18	£6.15	£2.02
19	£6.15	£1.90
20	£106.15	£30.84
	Price	**£97.50**

At an interest rate of 6.375%, the present value of future cash flows equates to the current market price of £97.50. The cost of debt after tax is then:

6.375 x (1 – 0.23) = 4.91%

However, in the "real world", determining a company's cost of debt is far from straightforward, as it may have many bonds in issue, each with different coupons, different maturities and even denominated in different currencies.

The spreadsheet for this exercise can be found at https://www.liverpooluniversitypress.co.uk/pages/essentials-of-financial-management-efm. Please ensure you click on Section 6 and the 6.2 tab at the bottom of the spreadsheet.

6.3 The weighted average cost of capital

In section 2.7 above we showed how to calculate the cost of equity capital. However, many firms will have a mixed capital structure whereby the company is financed by a mix of equity (i.e. shares) and bonds. In order to appraise a project with a mixed capital structure, it is essential to use the company's weighted average cost of capital, more commonly known as the WACC.

The WACC, K_{WACC}, can be found using:

$$K_{WACC} = K_E \left[\frac{MV(E)}{MV(E) + MV(D)}\right] + K_{DAT} \left[\frac{MV(D)}{MV(E) + MV(D)}\right]$$

where K_E is the cost of equity, K_{DAT} is the cost of debt after tax, MV(D) is the market value of debt and MV(E) is the market value of equity.

The equation, in the presence of preference shares, is as follows:

$$K_{WACC} = K_E \left[\frac{MV(E)}{MV(E) + MV(D) + MV(P)}\right]$$
$$+ K_{DAT} \left[\frac{MV(D)}{MV(E) + MV(D) + MV(P)}\right]$$
$$+ K_P \left[\frac{MV(P)}{MV(E) + MV(D) + MV(P)}\right]$$

where K_P is the cost of preference share capital and MV(P) is the market value of preference shares.

Often you are not provided with the market value of debt or equity but instead are provided with the ratio of debt to equity, in which case the above equation can be transformed as follows:

$$K_{WACC} = K_E \left[\frac{MV(E)}{MV(E) + MV(D)} \right] + K_{DAT} \left[\frac{MV(D)}{MV(E) + MV(D)} \right]$$

Dividing each term in brackets by MV(E):

$$K_{WACC} = K_E \left[\frac{MV(E)/MV(E)}{\frac{MV(E)+MV(D)}{MV(E)}} \right] + K_{DAT} \left[\frac{MV(D)/MV(E)}{\frac{MV(E)+MV(D)}{MV(E)}} \right]$$

$$K_{WACC} = K_E \left[\frac{1}{1 + \frac{MV(D)}{MV(E)}} \right] + K_{DAT} \left[\frac{MV(D)/MV(E)}{1 + \frac{MV(D)}{MV(E)}} \right]$$

$$K_{WACC} = \left[K_E + K_{DAT} \times \frac{MV(D)}{MV(E)} \right] \left[1 + \frac{MV(D)}{MV(E)} \right]$$

or simply using D/E to denote the MV(D)/MV(E):

$$K_{WACC} = \left[K_E + K_{DAT} \times {}^D/_E \right] \left[1 + {}^D/_E \right]$$

The debt to equity ratio (D/E) measures the market value of debt divided by the market value of equity. The former is simply the sum of the present value of all outstanding bonds and the latter is the number of shares in issue multiplied by the current market price. Many financial websites report this ratio.

Example

You are given the following information regarding the financing of a company:

K_E = 20%; MV(E) = £10m

K_{DAT} = 6%; MV(D) = £4m

K_P = 10%; MV(P) = £1m

The company is considering a project that requires an investment of £5m, which generates a return of £5.78m after one period. Should the project be accepted?

The first step is to calculate the WACC:

K_{WACC} = 20%(10/15) + 6%(4/15) + 10%(1/15) = 15.6%

The project requires an investment of £5m and therefore, given the capital structure:

debt holders invest 4/15ths

preference holders invest 1/15th

shareholders invest 10/15ths

Given each of their required returns, we obtain the following:

Financing	%	Amount	Required return
Debt holders	26.67%	£1,333,333.33	£1,413,333.33
Preference shareholders	6.67%	£333,333.33	£366,666.67
Ordinary shareholders	66.67%	£3,333,333.33	£4,000,000
	100%	£5,000,000	£5,780,000

If we evaluate this simple project at the WACC we obtain:

r	15.6%	
Time	0	1
CF	−£5,000,000	+£5,780,000
PV	−£5,000,000	+£5,000,000
NPV	£0	

The NPV of this project is zero; however, the project generates a return of £5,780,000, which satisfies the demands of the providers of capital, and therefore the project should be accepted.

6.4 Bringing this all together

You have been asked to calculate the WACC for Hart plc and have been provided with the following market data:

Hart plc has one bond in issue expiring in eight years, paying no coupon, with a par value of £1,000 and is currently priced at £721.76.

beta = 1.2, risk-free rate = 2% p.a., historical market-risk premium = 5.5% p.a.

Assuming that the ratio of debt to equity is 2:1 and that the corporate tax rate is 23%, find the WACC for Hart plc.

Cost of debt

K_d is the r that solves:

$$721.76 = \frac{1,000}{(1 + r)^8}$$

$$(1 + r)^8 = \frac{1,000}{721.76} \Rightarrow r = \sqrt[8]{\frac{1,000}{721.76}} = 0.0416 = 4.16\%$$

As the tax rate is 23% then:

$K_{dat} = 4.16 \times (1 - 0.23) = 3.20\%$

Cost of equity

$K_E = 2 + 1.2 \times 5.5 = 8.6\%$

WACC

$$K_{WACC} = \left[K_E + K_{DAT} \times \frac{D}{E} \right] / \left[1 + \frac{D}{E} \right]$$

$$K_{WACC} = \frac{[8.6\% + 3.2\% \times 2]}{[1 + 2]} = 5\%$$

Hart plc is considering an investment of £2.5m that is expected to produce an annual net cash flow of £0.5m for the next eight years. Evaluate this project using NPV, IRR, payback and modified payback. Hart plc requires a payback of four years.

r	5.%								
Years	0	1	2	3	4	5	6	7	8
CF	−£2.5m	£0.5m	£0.5m	£0.5m	£0.5m	£0.5m	£0.5m	£0.5m	£0.5m
PV	−£2.5m	£0.48m	£0.45m	£0.43m	£0.41m	£0.39m	£0.37m	£0.36m	£0.34m
NPV	£0.73m								

The NPV is +£0.73m and therefore the project should be accepted.

In order to find the IRR we choose a higher r that produces a negative NPV.

r	15%								
Years	0	1	2	3	4	5	6	7	8
CF	−£2.5m	£0.5m	£0.5m	£0.5m	£0.5m	£0.5m	£0.5m	£0.5m	£0.5m
PV	−£2.5m	£0.43m	£0.38m	£0.33m	£0.29m	£0.25	£0.22m	£0.19m	£0.16m
NPV	−£0.26m								

$IRR = 5\% + (15\% - 5\%) \times (0.73)/(0.73 + |0.26|) = 12.37\%$

As the WACC is 5% then, on the basis of IRR, this project should be accepted.

In order to find the simple payback, we examine the cumulative cash flows:

Years	0	1	2	3	4	5	6	7	8
CF	−£2.5m	£0.5m	£0.5m	£0.5m	£0.5m	£0.5m	£0.5m	£0.5m	£0.5m
Cumulative CF	−£2.5m	−£2m	−£1.5m	−£1m	−£0.5m	£0m	£0.5m	£1m	£1.5m

It is evident that this project pays back after five years. As Hart plc requires a payback of four years, then, on the basis of simple payback, this project is rejected.

In order to find the modified payback we examine the cumulative PV of cash flows:

r	5%								
Years	0	1	2	3	4	5	6	7	8
CF	−£2.5m	£0.5m	£0.5m	£0.5m	£0.5m	£0.5m	£0.5m	£0.5m	£0.5m
PV	−£2.5m	£0.48m	£0.45m	£0.43m	£0.41m	£0.39m	£0.37m	£0.36m	£0.34m
Cumulative PV	−£2.5m	−£2.02m	−£1.57m	−£1.14m	−£0.73m	−£0.34m	£0.04m	£0.39m	£0.73m

It is evident that the PVs recover the investment some time in year 6. The modified payback is therefore:

$$5 + |0.34|/0.37 = 5.9 \text{ years.}$$

As Hart plc requires a payback of four years, on the basis of modified payback, this project is rejected.

The spreadsheet for this exercise can be found at https://www.liverpooluniversitypress.co.uk/pages/essentials-of-financial-management-efm. Please ensure you click on Section 6 and the 6.4a and 6.4b tabs at the bottom of the spreadsheet.

Activity 6.1

You have been asked to calculate the WACC for Debreu plc and have been provided with the following market data:

beta = 2, risk-free rate = 2% p.a., historical market-risk premium = 4% p.a.

Debreu plc has one bond in issue expiring in five years, paying no coupon, with a par value of £1,000 and is currently priced at £610.

Assuming that the ratio of debt to equity is 1:1 and that the corporate tax rate is 23%, find the WACC for Debreu plc.

7
Foreign exchange risk

7.1 Exchange-rate risk and exchange-rate regimes

In Chapter 6 we introduced a technique to find a discount rate that is commensurate with the riskiness of future cash flows. This discount reflects investors' impatience to consume, inflation and uncertainty over future cash flows. When a company is trading internationally a further risk needs to be considered – transaction exposure. Transaction exposure is the risk faced by companies that trade internationally, when exchange rates change after a company has entered into an agreement, leading to higher domestic currency costs or lower domestic currency revenue.

However, different countries operate various exchange-rate regimes. Below we detail the exchange-rate regime for (i) China, (ii) the Czech Republic, (iii) France, (iv) the UK and (v) the United Arab Emirates.

China

China officially maintains a de jure managed floating exchange rate arrangement with a view to keeping the RMB exchange rate stable at an adaptive and equilibrium level based on market supply and demand with reference to a basket of currencies to preserve the stability of the Chinese economy and financial markets. The floating band of the RMB's trading prices is 2% against the U.S. dollar in the interbank foreign exchange market—i.e., on each business day, the trading prices of the RMB against the U.S. dollar in the market may fluctuate within a band of ±2% around the midrate released that day by China's Foreign Exchange Trading System (CFETS).[1]

Czech Republic

The de jure exchange rate arrangement is floating. The external value of the koruna is determined by supply and demand in the interbank foreign exchange market, in which the Czech National Bank (CNB) participates.[2]

France

The de jure exchange rate arrangement of the euro area is free floating. France participates in a currency union (EMU) with, as of January 1, 2015, 18 other members (previously 17) of the EU and has no separate legal tender. The euro, the common currency, floats freely and independently against other currencies.[3]

United Kingdom

The de jure and de facto exchange rate arrangements are free floating. The exchange rate of the pound sterling is determined on the basis of supply and demand in the foreign exchange market.[4]

United Arab Emirates

The de jure exchange rate arrangement is a conventional peg. The dirham was pegged to the U.S. dollar in 1980. A January 2003 decision made the peg official. The dirham is pegged to the U.S. dollar, the intervention currency, at the midrate of Dh 3.6725 per dollar (1 dirham = US$0.2723).[5]

Hence, the extent to which a company has exposure to exchange-rate risk depends upon which country it is trading with.

---

[1] 2016 Annual Report on Exchange Arrangements and Exchange Restrictions International Monetary Fund, P. 750, https://www.imf.org/en/Publications/Annual-Report-on-Exchange-Arrangements-and-Exchange-Restrictions/Issues/2017/01/25/Annual-Report-on-Exchange-Arrangements-and-Exchange-Restrictions-2016-43741
[2] 2016 Annual Report, P. 1006.
[3] 2016 Annual Report, P. 1237.
[4] 2016 Annual Report, P. 3595.
[5] 2016 Annual Report, P. 3580.

In the language of the FX market, it is convention to use the terms 'appreciation' and 'depreciation' rather than 'rise' and 'fall'. For example, if we consider the exchange rate between the US dollar and the pound sterling, the exchange rate fell from US$1.4558/GBP on 24 June 2016 (the day after the EU referendum) to US$1.2288/GBP at the end of 2016. Since one pound now buys fewer US dollars, we say that the pound has depreciated. In contrast, it now requires fewer US dollars to buy pounds and hence we say that the dollar has appreciated.

In November 2012, the exchange rate between the Japanese yen and the US dollar was 82.15 JPY/US$1. In October 2017, it was 112.39 JPY/US$1. Hence the JPY has depreciated, as more JPY are required to buy US$1. Likewise, the US dollar has appreciated, as US$1 buys more JPY in 2017 than it did in 2012.

7.2 How big is the foreign exchange market?

When one hears the word "market" one typically thinks of a physical location, especially as stock exchanges and futures exchanges were once exciting and vibrant places to visit. However, nowadays the vast majority of trades are matched electronically rather than by what was known as open outcry. By contrast, the foreign exchange market has never resided in a physical location and has always relied upon technology to facilitate transactions. In fact the US dollar/GBP exchange rate is still referred to as Cable in deference to a time when the rate was transmitted via cable along the bottom of the Atlantic Ocean. While nowadays, with the advent of electronic trading, most financial markets operate 24 hours a day, the foreign exchange market has long been open beyond traditional business hours due to the overlapping of time zones. Apart from public holidays and weekends, there is nearly always one financial centre open. Foreign exchange activity is carried out in all financial centres around the world, though some centres are more important than others. According to the Bank for International Settlements' triennial survey (2016), 36.9% of activity takes place in the UK, followed by 19.5% in the United States, 7.9% in Singapore and 6.7% in Hong Kong.[6]

---

[6] Bank for International Settlements Triennial Central Bank Survey 2016, p. 14, http://www.bis.org/publ/rpfx16fx.pdf

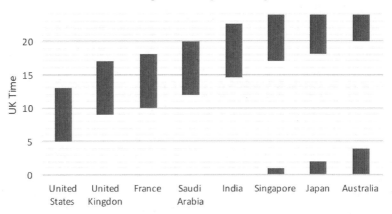

This diagram summarises the unique nature of the foreign exchange market. It is evident that the United Kingdom's trading times overlap with the United States, mainland Europe, the Middle East and India. This, and the use of English, partially explains the UK's dominant share of daily foreign exchange turnover.

As the FX market is not in one physical location, it is not easy to quantify the size of the market. However, every three years the Bank for International Settlements (BIS) conducts a triennial survey. The findings of the April 2016 survey stated "Trading in foreign exchange markets averaged $5.1 trillion per day in April 2016. This is down from $5.4 trillion in April 2013, a month which had seen heightened activity in Japanese yen against the background of monetary policy developments at that time."[7]

The same survey found that in 2016 the following currencies were most dominant:

USD – 87%
EUR – 33.4%
JPY – 23.1%
GBP – 11.8%

As two currencies are involved in each transaction, the sum of shares in individual currencies will total 200%. Therefore, out of every 200 transactions, approximately 155 involved just four currencies: USD, EUR, JPY and GBP. In fact, of these 200 transactions, the same survey

[7] Bank for International Settlements Triennial Central Bank Survey 2016, p. 3, http://www.bis.org/publ/rpfx16fx.pdf

concluded that 24.1% involved the USD against the EUR, which makes this the most important currency pair.[8]

7.3 Spot and forward markets and currency quotations

Buying a currency at the spot exchange implies "immediate" delivery and payment. At the time of writing, the spot quotation for the USD against the GBP was:

1.3182 – 1.3184 US$/GBP

The way to interpret this is as follows: 1 GBP would buy US$1.3182, whereas if you had USD and wanted 1 GBP you would need to give up US$1.3184. Ask yourself, why could you not buy USD at 1.3184 and sell USD at 1.3182? If this was the case and I had £1m available I could buy:

US$1.3184/GBP x 1m GBP = US$1,318,400

which I could sell back at US$1.3182/GBP:

US$1,318,400/1.3182 = £1,000,151.71

As you finish with more than you started with, you clearly cannot buy USD at the right-hand price and sell at the left. In fact, using the quotes in the correct manner, if you start with £1m you would end up with £999,848.30.

Earlier it was noted that in April 2016, 155 out of 200 transactions involved the USD, GBP, JPY or EUR. What then about a company wishing to exchange Thai bhat for Indonesian rupiah? How do we determine this exchange rate? A cross-exchange rate is defined as an exchange rate between two currencies which is derived from their common relationship with a third currency. As the majority of currencies are only quoted against the USD, GBP, EUR and JPY, we can obtain any cross-exchange rate by using the two currencies' exchange rate against one of these currencies.

Consider this analogy:

If one pound buys 8 apples and one pound also buys 4 oranges, what is the relative value of apples to oranges? Clearly it is 1 orange = 2 apples.

At the time of writing, the exchange rate between the Indonesian rupiah and the USD was 13,504 IDR/USD, and the exchange rate between the Thai bhat and the USD was 33.10

---

[8] Bank for International Settlements Triennial Central Bank Survey 2016, p. 5, http://www.bis.org/publ/rpfx16fx.pdf

THB/USD. Using the apples and oranges analogy from above, the exchange rate between the Indonesian rupiah and the Thai bhat is then:

13,504/33.10 = 407.98 IDR per THB.

This is the cross-exchange rate.

What if a trader was instead quoting 450 IDR per THB? What opportunities would exist for an investor with US$1m?

IDR/USD rate	13,503 IDR/USD
THB/USD rate	33.1 THB/USD
IDR/THB=	450 IDR/THB
Investor	US$1,000,000
Convert to THB	THB33,100,000 @ 33.1 THB/USD
Convert to IDR	IDR14,895,000,000 @ 450 IDR/THB
Convert to USD	US$1,103,088.20 @ 13,503 IDR/USD
Profit	**US$103,088.20**
Profit	**10.31%**

Hence an arbitrage profit of 10.31% can be earned by converting the USD to THB and then to IDR and then back to USD. This is known as triangular arbitrage. Once the exchange rate returns to 407.95 INR/THB, the arbitrage opportunity disappears.

There also exists a forward market where deals are for future delivery – usually one, three or six months' ahead, although other durations are possible provided that the market in the currency has sufficient volume. Forward rates are used by companies to hedge against exchange risk. For example, if I have a payment of Japanese yen to make in three months' time, I might prefer to agree the price now rather being exposed to an appreciation of the JPY vis-à-vis the GBP. Likewise, if I am receiving CHF in six months' time, I may prefer to agree the price now rather than be exposed to a depreciation in the value of the CHF vis-à-vis the GBP. Arranging to buy (or sell) at a price agreed now, but for delivery in the future to avoid exchange rate risk, is known as hedging.

Example

Consider a UK firm that has outsourced part of its manufacturing process to the Czech Republic. It must pay an invoice for 2.5m CZK in three months' time. What exchange rate risk does it face and how can the company hedge this risk?

An appreciation of the CZK would mean that the company would have to pay more GBP to obtain the 2.5m CZK in three months' time. To hedge this risk, the company could arrange to buy the 2.5m CZK at a price agreed now, but for delivery in the future.

At the time of writing the CZK/GBP spot rate was 28.6970 and the CZK/GBP three-month forward rate was 28.7651.

Exposure	2,500,000 Kč	
Three months' forward rate	28.7651 CZK/GBP	
Potential spot rate (CZK/GBP)	**Unhedged cost**	**Forward cost**
24	£104,166.67	£86,910.87
25	£100,000.00	£86,910.87
26	£96,153.85	£86,910.87
27	£92,592.59	£86,910.87
28	£89,285.71	£86,910.87
29	£86,206.90	£86,910.87
30	£83,333.33	£86,910.87
31	£80,645.16	£86,910.87
32	£78,125.00	£86,910.87
33	£75,757.58	£86,910.87
34	£73,529.41	£86,910.87

Whatever happens, the company is locked into a cost of £86,910.87. If the CZK depreciates (i.e. the rate > 28.7651), the company might wish, in hindsight, that it had not hedged.

Example

Consider a UK firm that is to receive CHF 100m from an asset sale in Geneva in three months' time. What exchange rate risk does it face? The three-month forward rate is 1.2775 CHF/GBP. Evaluate this hedge at spot rates of 1.2, 1.25, 1.3, 1.35 and 1.4 CHF/GBP.

The firm is worried about a depreciation of the CHF which would mean that it received less GBP than anticipated. To hedge this risk, the company could arrange to sell the 100m CHF at a price agreed now, but for delivery in the future.

Exposure	CHF100,000,000	
Three-month forward rate=	1.2775 CHF/GBP	
Potential spot rate (CHF/GBP)	**Unhedged revenue**	**Forward revenue**
1.2	£83,333,333.33	£78,277,886.50
1.25	£80,000,000	£78,277,886.50
1.3	£76,923,076.92	£78,277,886.50
1.35	£74,074,074.07	£78,277,886.50
1.4	£71,428,571.43	£78,277,886.50

Whatever happens, the company is locked into a revenue of £78,277,886.50. If the CHF appreciates (i.e. the rate < 1.2775), the company might wish, in hindsight, that it had not hedged.

The spreadsheet for this exercise can be found at https://www.liverpooluniversitypress.co.uk/pages/essentials-of-financial-management-efm. Please ensure you click on Section 7 and the 7.3a, 7.3b and 7.3c tabs at the bottom of the spreadsheet.

7.4 Calculating the forward rate

The forward rate between two currencies is not, in contrast to the spot rate, determined by the forces of supply and demand. Instead, it is determined by adjusting the spot rate according to the interest differential. It also draws upon the concept of no arbitrage. Arbitrage is an action taken by an investor whereby a positive return can be earned without bearing any risk. As detailed in Chapter 2, if no risk is borne then the maximum return should be the risk-free rate.

Let us assume that 12-month US interest rates were 5% per annum, 12-month UK interest rates were 2% per annum, the spot rate is US$1.5/GBP and the 12-month USD/GBP forward rate is US$1.56/GBP. A UK investor could then borrow £1m, convert to USD at US$1.5/GBP, invest at the higher US interest rate of 5% for 12 months, while simultaneously selling the proceeds forward at US$1.56/GBP. The outcome would be:

Borrow	£1,000,000
Convert to USD	$1,500,000
Invest in USD	$1,575,000
Sell forward	£1,009,615.38

| Repay loan | £1,020,000 |
| Profit | −£10,384.62 |

Hence, if the forward rate was 1.56 USD per GBP there appears to be no arbitrage opportunity to borrow GBP's, convert to USD's, invest in USD's whilst simultaneously selling the proceeds forward. However, clearly the forward market is not in equilibrium as if it were the profit should be zero. Considering instead an arbitrage of borrowing USD, converting to GBP, investing in GBP whilst simultaneously selling the proceeds forward we obtain:

Borrow	$1,000,000
Convert to GBP	£666,666.67
Invest in GBP	£680,000
Sell forward	$1,060,800
Repay loan	$1,050,000
Profit	$10,800

If the forward rate was instead US$1.5441/GBP, the arbitrage opportunity would disappear. In the first example, 1.56 US dollars were required to sell forward for each pound, while in the second case 1.53 US dollars were required to sell forward for each pound. However, if 1.5441 US dollars are required, then the proceeds from selling US dollars forward are just sufficient to repay the loan and the arbitrage opportunity disappears.

Consider an investor who borrows A GBP at a rate of i_{UK} for 12 months. They could convert these GBP into US dollars at S($/£) to obtain:

$$A \times S(\$/£)$$

which they could invest at i_{US} for 12 months to earn:

$$A \times S(\$/£) \times (1 + i_{US})$$

which they could then sell forward at $F_{12/12}(\$/£)$ to produce the following GBP amount:

$$\frac{A \times S(\$/£) \times (1 + i_{US})}{F_{12/12}(1 + i_{UK})}$$

To preclude arbitrage:

$$\frac{A \times S(\$/£) \times (1 + i_{US})}{F_{12/12}(\$/£)} = A \times (1 + i_{US})$$

This can be rearranged thus:

$$F_{12/12}(\$/£) = \frac{S(\$/£) \times (1 + i_{US})}{(1 + i_{US})}$$

Note that the "As" cancel out:

Hence for the example above:

$$F_{12/12}(\$/£) = \frac{1.5 \times (1 + 0.05)}{(1 + 0.02)} = 1.5441 \; USD \; per \; GBP$$

Equivalent equations exist to calculate the one-month, three-month and six-month forward rates:

$$F_{1/12}(\$/£) = \frac{S(\$/£) \times \left(1 + \frac{i_{US}}{12}\right)}{\left(1 + \frac{i_{US}}{12}\right)}$$

$$F_{3/12}(\$/£) = \frac{S(\$/£) \times \left(1 + \frac{i_{US}}{4}\right)}{\left(1 + \frac{i_{US}}{4}\right)}$$

$$F_{6/12}(\$/£) = \frac{S(\$/£) \times \left(1 + \frac{i_{US}}{2}\right)}{\left(1 + \frac{i_{US}}{2}\right)}$$

Example

If the three-month US interest rate is 1% p.a., the three-month South African interest rate is 6% p.a. and the South African rand (ZAR) exchange rate to the USD is 13.50 ZAR per USD, then what is the three-month forward rate?

Here we need to modify the equation above in the light of the new currency:

$$F_{3/12}(ZAR/USD) = \frac{S(ZAR/USD) \times \left(1 + \frac{i_{ZAR}}{4}\right)}{\left(1 + \frac{i_{US}}{4}\right)} = \frac{13.5 \times \left(1 + \frac{.06}{4}\right)}{\left(1 + \frac{.01}{4}\right)}$$

$$= 13.6683 \; ZAR/USD$$

The spreadsheet for this exercise can be found at https://www.liverpooluniversitypress.co.uk/pages/essentials-of-financial-management-efm. Please ensure you click on Section 7 and the 7.4a and 7.4b tabs at the bottom of the spreadsheet.

Activity 7.1

The spot rate between the Danish krona and the euro is 7.4422 DKK/EUR. The 12-month euro and Danish krona interest rates are 1.22% p.a. and 1.6% p.a. respectively. What would the 12-month DKK/EUR forward rate be?

8

An introduction to futures trading and hedging using futures

8.1 Introduction to futures

In section 7.2 we covered forward contracts that allowed a company to remove exchange-rate risk by agreeing a price now for delivery (or receipt) in the future. These contracts are traded over the counter and are a private transaction between the company and the bank. Now imagine if a company had agreed to buy a currency at a certain price and the exchange rate had moved in an advantageous direction. The forward contract could be considered to have value, but it is impossible to release this value. Futures contracts solve this problem.

A futures contract is a "marketable" forward contract, with marketability provided through futures exchanges that list hundreds of standardised contracts, establish trading rules, and provide clearing houses to guarantee and intermediate contracts. Futures contracts, like forward contracts, are a binding agreement to buy or sell an underlying asset at a specified date in the future. However, they primarily differ from forward contracts in that (i) the agreement can be sold and (ii) futures contracts are available on a much wider array of assets.

Futures contracts are traded on a centrally regulated exchange, with every negotiated price being "heard" by other traders. Traditionally, futures were traded via open outcry but more recently there has been a shift to electronic trading. In fact, on 2 July 2015, the leading futures exchange in the world, the Chicago Mercantile Exchange (CME), switched exclusively to electronic trading as a consequence of open outcry futures volumes declining to 1 per cent of daily futures volume.

8.2 Futures positions

In a long futures position, you agree to buy the contract's underlying asset at a specified price, with payment and delivery to occur on the expiration date (also referred to as the delivery date). In a short position, you agree to sell an asset at a specific price, with delivery and payment occurring at expiration. Thus far this sounds very similar to a forward contract. However, the real attraction of futures contracts over forward contracts is the ease of closing out a position. In order to close out a futures position, you simply need to do the reverse of whatever you did to get in to it. If you are long in a contract, then going short on the same contract (at the same exchange) will "cancel the contract". If you are short then going long will "cancel the position". Of course, the promises to sell and the promises to buy are likely to have been made at different prices so there will be a positive or negative cash flow determined by the relative prices. If you stop a futures contract prior to the end of trading on the last trade date, you are not obliged to buy or deliver anything.

Futures contracts can be used to speculate or to remove risk (referred to as hedging). When you speculate, you instigate a futures trade that will profit from your future market view. That is, if you think the market will rise you go long (buy) and if you think the market will fall you go short (sell). Alternatively, imagine that you would suffer some loss if the market fell. You could also go short on the futures to cover this risk. So, if the market falls you suffer a loss on the spot sale but gain on the future. This is referred to as hedging. Of course, a corporation could suffer a loss if the market rises, in which case they could take a long position on futures to cover this risk. Again, the loss would be offset by a gain on the future.

At the time of writing, the data for gold for the available contracts were:

Month	Last	Prior settle	Volume
Dec 2015	1062.4	1064.7	104
Jan 2016	1061.6	1063.7	296
Feb 2016	1061.5	1063.4	88,528
April 2016	1062.0	1064.1	1,090
June 2016	1062.2	1064.7	756

That is, trading takes place in the current month (December 2015), the next two calendar months (January and February 2016) and any April and any June.

Hence if you went long on the December 2015 contract at a price of $1,062.4 per troy ounce, you would acquire the obligation to buy 100 troy ounces of gold on the delivery date. If you went short you would acquire the obligation to sell 100 troy ounces of gold (of minimum 995 fineness) at a price of $1,062.4 per troy ounce by the delivery date. Note that the largest volume is for the contract within the February, April, August and October cycle.

The furthest contract maturity in December 2015 was for the contract expiring in December 2021, that is, 72 months (6 years) away.

8.3 Delivery

A final feature of futures contracts to be considered is the delivery (or settlement) process. Most open futures positions are closed out before delivery by taking out an offsetting position (e.g. the seller of a contract buys an equivalent position), but the delivery process is important in ensuring that the futures price converges on the spot price on the delivery date.

If it were not for the possibility of physical delivery of the underlying cash market good by the seller of the futures contract to the buyer, there would be no mechanism to guarantee convergence of futures and spot prices. For example, at any time prior to expiration, the futures price is merely a promise to do something in the future, but on the day the contract expires it is no longer a promise to do something in the future but to do something that day.

Example

If the spot price of gold is $1,250 per troy ounce and the futures price, for delivery in three months, is $1,300 per troy ounce, it is tempting to think that an investor could buy gold in the spot market now, and simultaneously enter into a short futures position to sell the gold at the higher price and realise a profit of $50 per troy ounce. However, the investor would need to have the cash available to purchase the gold in the spot market, thus forgoing interest (opportunity cost) and would then need to store, insure and ship the gold to the required location to fulfil the terms of the futures contract. All of these costs, aside from the delivery cost, are proportional to time and will eat into, if not eliminate, any potential profit. However, if these prices existed on the delivery date of the contract then only the shipping costs would remain, and these would likely to be small relative to the size of the transaction as a whole.

8.4 Minimum performance bond requirements

Consider two investors who have differing views on the future direction of the price of corn. Investor A believes that the price of corn will rise and instigates a long position of 10 contracts. Investor B believes that the price of corn will fall and instigates a short position of 10 contracts. The face value of each contract is 5,000 bushels.

It would be rather clumsy if investor A had to deal directly with investor B, since if either investor wished to close the position before the other, they would have to establish an offsetting position with a third investor. To overcome this, futures exchanges use clearing houses that guarantee each contract and act as an intermediary by breaking up each contract after the trade has been instigated.

If in the example above the corn futures positions are established at 350 cents per bushel and the price moved to 400 cents per bushel, then the profit/loss facing investor A and B would be:

Investor A: $10 \times 5,000 \times [400 - 350]/100 = +\$25,000$

Investor B: $-10 \times 5,000 \times [400 - 350]/100 = -\$25,000$

It follows that investor A's receiving their profit is dependent upon investor B. In order to guarantee fulfilment of these obligations, futures traders are required to deposit a performance bond, more commonly known as margin. There are three different types of margin: initial margin, maintenance margin and variation margin. The initial margin is an amount, per contract, that must be deposited when a futures contract is instigated.

At the end of each day, the profits/losses for each futures position are calculated. This in turn will change the balance of the margin account. The process of calculating the daily profit or loss on a futures position is known as "marking to market". If you have gone long (bought) a futures contract at a price $P(0)$, then at the end of the day there will be a positive or negative cash flow to your account in the amount of:

$[P(1)-P(0)] \times$ face value of the contract

where $P(1)$ is the settlement price at the end of the trading day.

If you go short (sell), the cash flows are the reverse of those above.

Margin requirements are in place to protect each counterpart in a futures contract, and logically they vary with the volatility of the underlying asset. As of 3 November 2017, the maintenance margin on corn futures, traded on the Chicago Mercantile Exchange (CME), was US$750 per contract. It is convention at the CME to set the initial margin at 110% for speculators and 100% for hedgers.

In the corn futures example above, both investors, as speculators, would need to deposit:

$10 \times 1.1 \times \$750 = \$8,250$

If, via the marking to market process, the margin account falls below the maintenance margin level, then investors are required to top the margin account up to the initial margin level. The amount of cash paid is referred to as variation margin.

Each corn contract is for 5,000 bushels, which at 350 cents per bushel equates to $17,500. With initial margin set at $850, for speculators, this makes the initial margin equal to about 5%, which makes speculation using futures extremely attractive.

Example

Assume you are a speculator and on 2 October 2017 you go long (i.e. buy) ten December 2017 gold futures contracts at an opening price of $1,275.8 per troy ounce. Each contract has a face value of 100 troy ounces. There is an initial margin of $4,900 per contract.

Over the next few days the settlement prices are:

3 October – $1,274.6 per troy ounce

4 October – $1,277.5 per troy ounce

5 October – $1,270.6 per troy ounce

6 October – $1,278.9 per troy ounce

On 9 October you close the position at $1,284.6 per troy ounce.

What is the daily profit/loss and the total profit from 3 to 9 October? Would the investor be required to pay variation margin?

N = 10	FV = 100 troy ounces	Initial margin US$5,390 per contract	Maintenance margin US$4,900 per contract
Date	Price	P/L	Margin a/c
2/10/17	$1,275.80		$53,900.00
3/10/17	$1,274.60	–$1,200.00	$52,700.00
4/10/17	$1,277.50	$2,900.00	$55,600.00
5/10/17	$1,270.60	–$6,900.00	$48,700.00
6/10/17	$1,278.90	$8,300.00	$57,000.00
9/10/17	$1,284.60	$5,700.00	$62,700.00
		$8,800.00	

Due to the accumulated losses, the margin account, before any variation margin payments, would fall below the maintenance margin level at the end of 5 October 2017. The investor would then need to pay $5,200 of variation margin on 5 October 2017.

N = 10	FV = 100 troy ounces	Initial margin US$5,390 per contract	Maintenance margin US$4,900 per contract	
Date	Price	P/L	Margin a/c	Variation margin
2/10/17	$1,275.80		$53,900.00	
3/10/17	$1,274.60	−$1,200.00	$52,700.00	
4/10/17	$1,277.50	$2,900.00	$55,600.00	
5/10/17	$1,270.60	−$6,900.00	$53,900.00	$5,200.00
6/10/17	$1,278.90	$8,300.00	$62,200.00	
9/10/17	$1,284.60	$5,700.00	$67,900.00	
		$8,800.00		

Accumulated profit can be found using the initial price and the last price:

10 x 100 x [$1,284.60 - $1,275.80] = $8,800.

Note the final margin balance equals the initial margin plus accumulated profit and loss plus variation margin:

$53,900 + $8,800 + $5,200 = $67,900

The spreadsheet for this exercise can be found at https://www.liverpooluniversitypress.co.uk/pages/essentials-of-financial-management-efm. Please ensure you click on Section 8 and the 8.4 tab at the bottom of the spreadsheet.

8.5 Hedging with futures contracts

Futures contracts provide companies with the opportunity to remove the risk associated with a rise in input costs or a decrease in revenue.

For example, a company that is exposed to a rise in the price of raw materials could use futures contracts to remove this risk. This would be referred to as a long hedge. In a long hedge, the company takes a long position in the futures contract and, on the assumption that the spot price and the futures prices are positively correlated, as the spot price rises, and hence the cost of the raw materials, the futures price will also rise. If the hedge is successful, then the profit from the long futures position will offset the increase in the cost of the raw materials.

A company that is exposed to a fall in revenue, associated with a decline in the selling price of an asset in the spot market, could also use futures contracts to remove risk. This would be referred to as a short hedge. In a short hedge, the company takes a short position in the futures contract and as the spot price falls, the futures price will also fall. If the hedge is successful, then the profit from the short futures position will offset the decrease in revenue from selling the asset in the spot market.

In both long hedges and short hedges, if the underlying movement in the asset price is favourable, then the reduced costs or increased revenue will be cancelled out by a loss on the futures position.

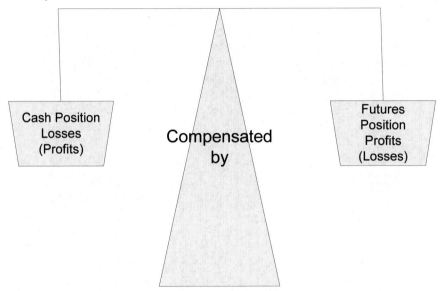

In a long hedge, any increased costs (and hence losses) from buying at the spot price would be offset by a profit on the futures position. However, any reduced costs, resulting from a favourable movement in the spot price, would be offset by a loss on the futures position.

In a short hedge, any reduced revenue (and hence losses) from selling at the spot price would be offset by a profit on the futures position. However, any increased revenue, resulting from a favourable movement in the spot price, would be offset by a loss on the futures position.

Example

A classic example of exposure to a rise in the price of a raw material is an oil refinery. Oil refineries process crude oil into products such as heating oil and kerosene. Crude oil can therefore be considered as an input to an oil refinery's production process and, as with any input, the company will wish to avoid the risk of a price rise. One of the most heavily traded futures contracts are crude oil futures and therefore an oil refinery can instigate a long hedge, whereby if the price of crude oil goes up in the spot market, the price of crude oil futures will also rise and the profit from the futures position will offset the rise in the input costs of crude oil. However, if the spot price of crude oil falls, the benefit from this favourable movement will be offset by a loss on the futures position.

Consider the case of an oil refinery that anticipates purchasing 100,000 barrels of crude oil in December. Crude oil futures traded on the CME have a face value of 1,000 barrels. Therefore, the oil refinery would need to instigate a long hedge comprising of a long position in 100 December futures contracts.

In order to hedge this risk, the oil refinery purchases 100 December 2017 crude oil futures contracts at a price of $49.92 per barrel. The mechanics of the hedge is that any increased (decreased) costs incurred in buying the 100,000 barrels of oil at the spot price will be offset by a profit (loss) on the futures position. If we assume (i) that the futures trade and the spot purchase are two separate transactions and (ii) that the spot and futures prices are equal on the expiry of the option, then we arrive at the following outcomes.

Exposure = 100,000 barrels	FV = 1,000 barrels				
N = 100	F0 = $49.92				
Spot price	$40.00	$45.00	$50.00	$55.00	$60.00
Futures price	$40.00	$45.00	$50.00	$55.00	$60.00
Spot cost	$4,000,000	$4,500,000	$5,000,000	$5,500,000	$6,000,000
Futures P/L	−$992,000	−$492,000	$8,000	$508,000	$1,008,000
Net cost	$4,992,000	$4,992,000	$4,992,000	$4,992,000	$4,992,000
Net cost (per barrel)	$49.92	$49.92	$49.92	$49.92	$49.92

Thus, if the price of crude oil on the spot market is $60/bl at the delivery date, the refinery would pay $60/bl and make a profit of $10.08/bl by closing out the futures position, representing a total cost per barrel of $49.92 ($60 − $10.08). But if the price of crude oil is $40/bl, the refinery would pay $40/bl but would make a loss of $9.92 by closing out the futures position, representing a total cost per barrel of $49.92 ($40 + $9.92). Therefore, regardless of the spot price, the refinery pays $49.92/bl.

The spreadsheet for this exercise can be found at https://www.liverpooluniversitypress.co.uk/pages/essentials-of-financial-management-efm. Please ensure you click on Section 8 and the 8.5a tab at the bottom of the spreadsheet.

Example

Consider the case of a wheat farmer who anticipates selling 50,000 bushels of wheat in March. The farmer's worry is obviously that the price of wheat will continue to fall below its current level of 461 cents per bushel. With wheat futures listed on the CME, the farmer can minimise price risk by taking a short position in the March wheat futures contract. With the standard size on wheat futures of 5,000 bushels, the farmer would need to go short in 10 March wheat futures contracts to hedge the March spot sale.

In order to hedge this risk, the farmer sells 10 March 2018 wheat futures contracts at a price of 461 cents per bushel. The mechanics of the hedge is that any reduced (increased) revenue incurred in selling the 50,000 bushels of wheat at the spot price will be offset by a profit (loss) on the futures position. If we assume (i) that the futures trade and the spot purchase are two separate transactions and (ii) that the spot and futures prices are equal on the expiry of the option, then we arrive at the following outcomes.

Exposure = 50,000 bushels	FV = 5,000 bushels				
N = 10	F0 = 461 cents per bushel				
Spot price	340	400	460	520	580
Futures price	340	400	460	520	580
Spot revenue	$170,000	$200,000	$230,000	$260,000	$290,000
Futures P/L	$60,500	$30,500	$500	−$29,500	−$59,500
Net revenue	$230,500	$230,500	$230,500	$230,500	$230,500
Net revenue (per bushel)	$4.61	$4.61	$4.61	$4.61	$4.61

The spreadsheet for this exercise can be found at https://www.liverpooluniversitypress.co.uk/pages/essentials-of-financial-management-efm. Please ensure you click on Section 8 and the 8.5b tab at the bottom of the spreadsheet.

We can see then that if the farmer receives only $3.40/bu for each bushel, he or she realises a profit on the futures position of $1.21/bu, resulting in net receipts of $4.61/bu. When the farmer receives $5.80, the futures position realises a loss of $1.19/bu, resulting in net receipts of $4.61/bu. Thus, regardless of the spot price, the farmer receives $4.61 per bushel.

The long hedge and short hedge examples provided here are almost too good to be true, as there is a guaranteed cost, in the case of the long hedge, or a guaranteed revenue, in the case of the short hedge, regardless of the resultant spot price. In practice, hedges are less than perfect. Quantity risk results from the standardisation of futures contracts. For example, if the oil refinery needs to purchase 105,000 barrels of crude oil, then it would either need to purchase 100 contracts, thereby leaving 5,000 barrels unhedged, or purchase 101 contracts and be over-hedged. The preceding examples relied upon the spot and futures prices moving in perfect correlation. In reality this may not be the case. Each futures contract has clear stipulations on the specification of the asset that should be delivered if a futures position reaches delivery. For example, cotton futures traded on the International Commodity Exchange require cotton to be delivered that is "Strict Low Middling Staple Length: 1 2/32nd". If a company was using this contract to hedge a change in the price of cotton and the cotton they were purchasing was of a different quality, there would be no guarantee that the spot and futures prices would move in perfect correlation. This is referred to as quality risk. In section 8.4 the concept of delivery was covered. The convergence of the spot and futures prices on the delivery date introduces basis (or timing) risk. The "scales" diagram introduced earlier supposes that an increase in costs (decrease in revenue) is offset by a profit on the futures position. In order for this to occur, the relative change in the spot and futures prices must be equal. For example, if the movements of spot and futures prices is as shown below, and you were hedging against a decline in price using futures, it is evident that the decline in revenue would be much greater than the profit on the future. Likewise, if the prices rose (and converged together), then the increased revenue would not be entirely cancelled out by the loss on the futures position.

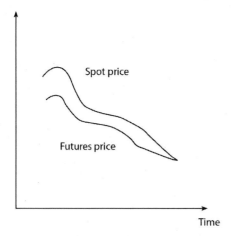

8.6 Basis

If the spot asset is sold or purchased at a date that differs from the expiration date, then the price on the futures contract will not necessarily be equal to the spot price. The difference between the futures price and the spot price is called the basis:

basis = spot price – futures price

The basis tends to narrow as expiration nears, converging to zero at the delivery date.

Under normal conditions, the futures price is higher than the cash price. Why? The futures price should incorporate the costs that the seller would incur for buying the commodity and storing it until delivery. These costs are called costs-of-carry.

The fair price of a future is then cash price + cost of carry.

If futures are fairly priced the basis will be negative, a position known as contango.

In exceptional circumstances, the opposite situation might occur and the cash price would be higher than the futures price. For example, this could be due to temporary scarcity of a commodity in the spot market causing an increase in the spot price. This situation is known as backwardation.

Consider the situation where a company knows that an asset will be sold, in the spot market, at some future date, t_1. In order to mitigate the risk of a price fall, the company instigates a short futures position at the futures price, F_0. If the resultant selling price is S_1 and the corresponding futures prices is F_1 then the net revenue from selling this asset is:

$$S_1 + [-(F_1 - F_0)]$$

If we define the basis at time t_1 as:

$$b_1 = S_1 - F_1$$

then the net revenue can be expressed as:

$$S_1 + (F_0 - F_1) = F_0 + b_1$$

The initial futures, price, F_0, is known when the hedge is instigated, but b_1 is not. Herein lies the uncertainty surrounding hedging and the so-called basis risk.

Example

Returning to the data in the previous wheat example, assume that the initial spot and futures prices are not equal. Previously we assumed that both the spot and futures prices were 461 cents per bushel. Now we will assume that the spot price is lower than the futures price at 420 cents per bushel. The basis is then –41 cents per bushel and we are in a situation of contango. If the spot price falls to 340 cents per bushel and the futures price drops to 350 cents per bushel, then we have the following outcome:

exposure = 50,000 bushels, face value = 5,000 bushels

number of contracts = 10

S_0 = 420 cents per bushel

$F_0 = 461$ cents per bushel

$S_1 = 340$ cents per bushel

$F_1 = 350$ cents per bushel

Therefore $b_1 = -10$ cents $= -\$0.1$

Revenue from selling wheat at S_1:

50,000 bushels x 340 cents per bushel $= \$170,000$

profit from futures position $= -10 \times 5,000 \times [350 - 461]/100 = \$55,500$

net revenue $= \$225,500$

net revenue per bushel $= \$4.51$ per bushel

Or $F_0 + b_1 = \$4.61 + (-\$0.1) = \$4.51$.

Exposure = 50,000 bushels	
N = 10	$F_0 = 461$ cents per bushel
FV = 5,000 bushels	$S_0 = 420$ cents per bushel
	$b_0 = -41$ cents per bushel
	$F_1 = 350$ cents per bushel
	$S_1 = 340$ cents per bushel
	$b_1 = -10$ cents per bushel
Spot revenue	$170,000
Profit/Loss from futures position	$55,500
Net revenue	$225,500
Net revenue (per bushel)	$4.51
Net revenue (per bushel)	$4.51 using formula

The spreadsheet for this exercise can be found at https://www.liverpooluniversitypress.co.uk/pages/essentials-of-financial-management-efm. Please ensure you click on Section 8 and the 8.6a tab at the bottom of the spreadsheet.

Note further that basis can lead to an improvement or worsening of a hedge. In our example it is worsened by 10 cents, but if the basis is reversed when the hedge is closed, and the market goes into backwardation, then the revenue would be increased.

Consider instead a situation where a company knows it will buy an asset at time t_1 and in order to avoid a rise in costs takes out a long futures position at time t_1. The price paid is S_1 and the profit on the futures position is then $(F_1 - F_0)$.

The effective price obtained for the asset with hedging is therefore:

$S_2 - (F_1 - F_0) = F_0 + b_1$ (note we subtract the profit on the futures position)

Example

Returning to the data in the oil refinery example, now assume that the initial spot and futures prices are not equal. Previously we assumed that both the spot and futures prices were $49.92 per barrel. Now we will assume that the spot price is lower than the futures price at $49.42 per barrel. The basis is then –$0.50 per barrel and we are in a situation of contango. If the futures price rises to $60 per barrel, and the spot price rises to $59.80 per barrel, then we have the following outcome:

$\quad$ exposure = 100,000 barrels, face value = 1,000 barrels

$\quad$ number of contracts = 100

$\quad$ $S_0 = 49.42$ $ per barrel

$\quad$ $F_0 = 49.92$ $ per barrel

$\quad$ $S_1 = 59.80$ $ per barrel

$\quad$ $F_1 = 60$ per barrel

Therefore $b_1 = -\$0.3$ per barrel

Cost of buying crude oil at S_1:

$\quad$ 100,000 barrels x $59.80 per barrel = $5,980,000

$\quad$ profit from futures position = + 100 x 1,000 x [60 – 49.92] = $1,008,000

$\quad$ net cost = $4,972,000

$\quad$ net cost per barrel = $49.72

Or $F_0 + b_1 = \$49.92 + (-\$0.2) = \$49.72$.

Exposure = 100,000 barrels	
N = 100	$F_0 = \$49.92$ per barrel
FV = 1,000 barrels	$S_0 = \$49.42$ per barrel
	$b_0 = -\$0.5$ per barrel
	$F_1 = \$60$ per barrel
	$S_1 = \$59.80$ per barrel

	$b_1 = -\$0.2$ per barrel
Spot cost	$5,980,000
Profit/Loss from futures position	$1,008,000
Net cost	$4,972,000
Net cost (per barrel)	$49.72
Net cost (per barrel)	$49.72 using formula

The spreadsheet for this exercise can be found at https://www.liverpooluniversitypress.co.uk/pages/essentials-of-financial-management-efm. Please ensure you click on Section 8 and the 8.6b tab at the bottom of the spreadsheet.

8.7 Hedge efficiency

In the previous two examples we have considered minimising net cost or maximising net revenue as the aim of the hedge. An alternative outlook is to consider the hedge efficiency:

$$Hedge\ Efficiency = \left| \frac{Gain\ or\ Loss\ on\ futures\ position}{Loss\ or\ Gain\ on\ spot\ position} \right|$$

It is usual to refer to the efficiency of a hedge as a percentage. The vertical lines indicate absolute values. Effectively we are measuring how much we were able to balance the scales shown earlier.

In the earlier wheat example, the initial spot price was 420 cents per bushel but the actual spot price was 340 cents per bushel. Had we been able to sell the wheat at 420 cents we would have realised revenue of $210,000, whereas we actually realised $170,000. In addition, the profit on our futures position was $55,500. It follows that the hedge efficiency is:

$$Hedge\ Efficiency = \left| \frac{+\$55,500}{\$170,000 - \$210,000} \right| = \frac{\$55.000}{-\$40,000} = 138.75\%$$

Here the spot price fell from 420 cents per bushel to 340 cents per bushel, a fall of 80 cents, but the futures price fell from 461 cents per bushel to 350 cents per bushel, a fall of 111 cents. It is evident that the fall in the spot price was less than the fall in the futures price, which explains why the hedge efficiency is greater than 100%.

Using our earlier notation, the hedge efficiency can also be found by the following equation:

$$1 + \frac{(b_0 - b_1)}{(S_1 - S_0)} = 1 + \frac{(-41 - (-10))}{(340 - 420)} = 1 + \frac{-31}{-80} = 138.75\%$$

Example

Consider the case of a wheat farmer who anticipates selling 50,000 bushels of wheat in March. The face value of wheat futures contracts traded on the CME is 5,000 bushels. What is the hedge efficiency using the following data?

> initial futures price = 420 cents per bushel
>
> initial basis = +15 cents per bushel
>
> final futures price = 350 cents per bushel
>
> final basis = 0 cents per bushel
>
> $F_0 = 420$, $S_0 = b_0 + F_0 = 15 + 420 = 435$
>
> $F_1 = 350$, $S_1 - b_1 + F_0 = 350 + 0 = 350$
>
> hedge efficiency = $1 + (15-0)/(350 - 435) = 1 + (15/-85) = 82.35\%$

Alternatively:

> expected revenue = $217,500
>
> actual revenue = $175,000
>
> change in revenue = -$42,500
>
> profit on futures position = $35,000
>
> hedge efficiency = $35,000/$42,500 = 82.35\%$

Activity 8.1

A food producer, Ohlin plc, expects to purchase 200,000 bushels of wheat in early September 2013. It wishes to hedge against the price risk by using wheat futures contracts traded on the CME, each with a face value of 5,000 bushels. The current price of September 2013 wheat futures traded on the CME is 872 cents per bushel and the current spot price is 862 cents per bushel. Evaluate this hedge in September 2013 assuming the following spot values (cents per bushel):

Spot price (cents per bushel	820	840	860	880	900	920	940

You may assume that the basis narrows to zero. What are the implications for the hedge efficiency if the basis remained constant?

8.8 Airlines hedging price risk

Consider an airline with a requirement to buy 100,000 metric tonnes of jet kerosene in February 2017 (assume it is now 29 July 2016). 100,000 metric tonnes is the equivalent of 793,000 barrels of oil. With 42 gallons in each barrel that is 33,306,000 gallons, and since a Boeing 777 jet burns fuel at 1,672 gallons an hour, this represents approximately 20,000 hours of flying time. Jet kerosene is produced in the process of refining crude oil. Therefore, as the price of crude oil goes up, the price of jet kerosene also rises. The chart below shows the rise (and fall) in prices of jet kerosene and crude oil during 2016 until 29 July. Note that the kerosene figure is scaled by a dividend of 7.93.

It is evident from the above that there exists a positive relationship between the two sets of data. This relationship is even more evident when we examine the relationship between the daily percentage changes in both prices.

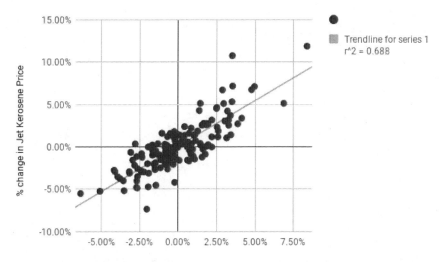

% change in Sept 2017 Crude Oil Futures Price

The r-squared value of 0.688 indicates how good a "fit" the trendline is. It is apparent that the majority of circles are in the north-east and south-west quadrants. If we take the square root of the r-squared figure we obtain the correlation between the two series as 0.829, which indicates strong positive correlation. It follows that to hedge the price risk of a rise in the price of jet kerosene, an airline could buy crude oil futures. Then, as the price of crude oil goes up, it will profit on its futures contracts and this will offset the associated increase in the price of jet kerosene.

On 29 July 2016, the price of a Brent crude oil futures contract expiring in September 2017 (it actually expired in July 2017) was $48.17/bl. The price of jet kerosene was $400 per metric tonne. Each crude oil futures contract is worth 1,000 barrels of oil. An airline would therefore need to buy 793 contracts (i.e. 793,000/1,000).

If the price of crude oil is higher in July 2017, then the airline will gain on the futures contracts. However, the price of jet kerosene will also have risen. Ideally, the increased cost of jet kerosene will be offset by a profit on the futures position. Alternatively, if the price of crude oil is lower in July 2017, then the airline will suffer a loss on the futures contracts. However, this will be cancelled out by a gain in buying the jet kerosene at a lower price. If crude oil and jet kerosene move in a 1-for-1 manner, then the increased (reduced) costs will be exactly cancelled out by a gain (loss) on the futures contracts.

On 31 July when the 2017 contract expired, the price of jet kerosene was $529 per metric tonne and the price of the crude oil future was $52.65 per barrel.

The outcome can then be evaluated as follows:

Exposure = 100,000 metric tonnes/ 793,000 barrels	
FV = 1,000 barrels	
N = 793	793
Expected cost (as of 29 July 2016)	$40,000,000
Actual cost (as of 31 July 2017)	$52,900,000
Change in cost	$12,900,000
P/L on future	$3,552,640
Hedge efficiency	27.54%
Effective cost	$49,347,360
Effective cost (per barrel)	$62.23

To use the basis analysis requires more work, as the spot price is in $ per metric tonne but the future is in $ per barrel. But if you divide the spot price by 7.93 then you can verify the effective price ($ per bl) as $F_0 + b_1$ and the hedge efficiency as $1 + [(b_0 - b_1)/(S_1 - S_0)]$

S_0 = $50.44 per barrel
F_0 = $48.17 per barrel
b_0 = $2.27 per barrel
S_1 = $66.71 per barrel
F_1 = $52.65 per barrel
b_1 = $14.06 per barrel
Effective cost = $F_0 + b_1$ = $62.23 per barrel
Hedge efficiency = $1 = [(b_0 - b_1)/(S_1 - S_0)]$ = 27.54%

This example illustrates that hedging in the real world is much more complicated than our stylised wheat and crude oil examples presented earlier. The undoing of the jet kerosene hedge was that rather than narrowing, the basis widened to $14.06 per barrel.

The spreadsheet for this exercise can be found at https://www.liverpooluniversitypress.co.uk/pages/essentials-of-financial-management-efm. Please ensure you click on Section 8 and the 8.8 tab at the bottom of the spreadsheet.

9
Introduction to options

9.1 Option terminology

Options are a unique type of financial contract that have a throwaway feature. They give you the right but not the obligation to do something. You only use the contract if you want to. This contrasts with forward contracts, which oblige you to make a transaction at the pre-agreed price even if the market has changed and you would rather not. The fact that options provide a right but not an obligation means that users are able to obtain insurance against an adverse movement in the price of an asset rate, while still retaining the opportunity to benefit from a favourable price movement. At the same time, the maximum risk to the buyer of an option is the actual cost of the option.

An American call option is an asset that gives its owner the right to purchase a given "asset" (e.g. some shares or a quantity of currency):

- at a predetermined price (the exercise or strike price)
- on, or before, a stated date (the expiration or maturity date).

An American put option is similar except that it gives the right to sell the "asset":

- at a predetermined price (the exercise or strike price)
- on, or before, a stated date (the expiration or maturity date).

In each option transaction there are two parties. The buyer of the option holds all the power and decides whether to buy, in the case of a call option, or to sell, in the case of a put option, the asset contained in the option contract. In contrast, the writer of the option stands ready to sell (if a call is exercised) or to buy (if a put is exercised). The maximum upside to the writer of the option is the premium received, and if they are forced to buy/sell it will only be because it is financially advantageous to the buyer.

The table below illustrates a typical equity option quotation:

Strike	Call			Put		
	T = 3 months	T = 6 months	T = 12 months	T = 3 months	T = 6 months	T = 12 months
80	$21.1	$22.5	$25.4	$0.1	$0.6	$1.5
85	$16.5	$18.3	$21.6	$0.4	$1.2	$2.5
90	$12.2	$14.4	$18.1	$1.1	$2.2	$3.8
95	$8.5	$11.1	$15.0	$2.4	$3.7	$5.4
100	$5.6	$8.3	$12.3	$4.4	$5.8	$7.5
105	$3.4	$6.0	$10.0	$7.1	$8.4	$9.9
110	$2.0	$4.2	$8.0	$10.6	$11.5	$12.7
115	$1.1	$2.9	$6.4	$14.6	$15.1	$15.8
120	$0.5	$2.0	$5.0	$19.1	$19.0	$19.2

These prices are generated using an asset price of $100, a standard deviation of 25% and interest rate of 5%, though what follows would apply regardless of the underlying assumptions.

It is evident that the further away the expiration of the option, the greater the option premium for both calls and puts. For example, the right to buy at $100 in 3 months' time is priced at $5.6, whereas the right to buy in 12 months' time is priced at $12.3. Similarly, the right to sell at $100 in 3 months' time is priced at $4.4, whereas the right to sell in 12 months' time is priced at $7.5.

Regardless of the maturity, it is clear from the table above that there is a positive relationship between put premiums and strike prices but a negative relationship between call premiums and strike prices. In Chapter 7 you were introduced to forward contracts, where there is one forward rate for each maturity. With options there is a "menu" to choose from, and as with all menus, the more attractive the offering, the more expensive it is. For example, it is clearly more attractive for an investor to buy at $80 in one year than at $120 in one year, and the premium ($25.4 versus $5) reflects this. Likewise, it is more attractive to sell at $120 in one year's time than at $80 in one year's time. Again, the premium reflects this ($19.2 versus $1.5).

The buyer of an option pays the premium of the option up front, and subsequently has the right to exercise or not exercise the option. Options can be purchased on an exchange (exchange-traded options) or direct from a bank (over-the-counter options, OTCs). Exchange-traded options are standardised in terms of expiration date and contract size. OTCs can be "tailor made" to suit your needs. For example, you can choose the expiration date, the amount to be bought or sold and the strike price.

9.2 Option strategies

Many types of option strategies exist, with exotic names such as straddles, strangles, butterflies, strips and straps. Strategies that combine options of the same type (i.e. all calls or all puts), but different strike prices and/or maturity dates, are referred to as spreads. Strategies that combine options of different type are referred to as combinations. All these strategies can be understood easily once you grasp the features of four fundamental option strategies:

- call and put purchases
- call and put writes

To best understand the features of these strategies, it is appropriate to examine the relationship between the price of the underlying asset, at expiration, and the net profit/loss.

9.3 Long call purchase

Consider an investor who buys a call option on ABC stock with an exercise price (X) of $100 at a call premium (C) of $6.25. In simple terms, this option gives the holder the right, but not the obligation, to buy ABC stock for $100. What we have to determine is what factors will lead to the option being exercised or thrown away.

If the stock price is $70 on the expiration date, will the investor exercise their call option? Of course not! Why would they buy the stock for $100 in the option market if they could buy it for $70 in the cash market? If the stock price is $80 on the expiration date will the investor exercise their call option? Again of course not. And so on for $81, $82 ... $99.

Note that, regardless of whether the option is exercised or not, the investor must still pay the premium of $6.25. However, if the stock price is $100 the investor is indifferent between buying the stock in the cash market and the options market.

What about stock prices above $100? At stock prices above $100, it is advantageous for the investor to buy the stock from the options contract rather than buying it in the cash market. However, as the investor paid $6.25 for the option, they are effectively paying $106.25 for the stock. So, although it is advantageous for the investor to exercise their option, in reality it would have been better not to have purchased the option at all. But if the stock price is above $106.25 at expiration, not only is it advantageous for the option to be exercised, it is in fact profitable. For example, if the stock price is $110 the investor could purchase the stock for $100 by the terms of the option contract, then sell the stock in the cash market for $110, thus making a profit of $10. The profit, net of the premium, is then $3.75. Following this logic, it is possible to map out a relationship between the stock price and profit/loss from exercising the option.

Call premium = $6.75

Call strike = $100

Terminal stock price	Exercise?	Premium	Profit from exercising	Net profit
80	No	$6.75	$0.00	−$6.75
85	No	$6.75	$0.00	−$6.75
90	No	$6.75	$0.00	−$6.75
95	No	$6.75	$0.00	−$6.75
100	Yes/No	$6.75	$0.00	−$6.75
105	Yes	$6.75	$5.00	−$1.75
110	Yes	$6.75	$10.00	$3.25
115	Yes	$6.75	$15.00	$8.25
120	Yes	$6.75	$20.00	$13.25
125	Yes	$6.75	$25.00	$18.25
130	Yes	$6.75	$30.00	$23.25

The spreadsheet for this exercise can be found at https://www.liverpooluniversitypress.co.uk/pages/essentials-of-financial-management-efm. Please ensure you click on Section 9 and the 9.3 tab at the bottom of the spreadsheet.

This relationship can best be described graphically. We refer to this relationship as a profit profile.

Net Profit vs. Terminal Stock Price for a Long Call

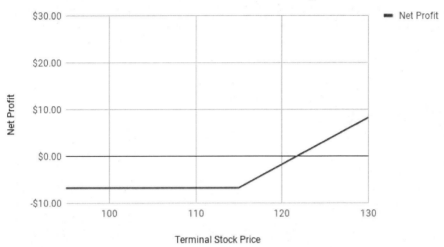

The profit profile highlights two important features of call purchases:

- The position provides an investor with unlimited profit potential.
- Losses are limited to an amount equal to the call premium.

These two features help explain why speculators prefer to buy a call rather than the stock itself. In addition, options are highly leveraged. In our example above, we have assumed that the price of ABC stock could range from $80 to $130 at expiration. If an investor purchased the stock for $100, the profit from the stock would range from –$20 to +$30, or in percentage terms from –20% to +30%. On the other hand, the return from the option would range from +344% to –100%. Thus, the potential reward to the speculator from buying a call instead of a stock can be substantial, 344% compared to 30%; but the potential loss is also large, –100% vs –20%. Note the profit of 344% is based on an investment in the option of $6.75 and the stock price rising to $130, earning a net profit of $23.25. As a long call is profitable following a price rise it is attractive to investors with a bullish view of the underlying asset.

9.4 Naked call write

The second fundamental option strategy involves the sale of a call in which the seller does not own the underlying stock. Such a position is known as a naked call write.

Again, assume that the exercise price on the call option on ABC stock is $100 and the call premium is $6.75. The profits/losses associated with each stock price from selling the call are depicted in the following table.

Call premium = $6.75				
Call strike = $100				
Terminal stock price	**Exercise?**	**Premium received**	**Action from writer**	**Net profit**
80	No	$6.75	Do nothing	$6.75
85	No	$6.75	Do nothing	$6.75
90	No	$6.75	Do nothing	$6.75
95	No	$6.75	Do nothing	$6.75
100	Yes/No	$6.75	Do nothing	$6.75
105	Yes	$6.75	Buy ABC at prevailing stock price, sell at $100	$1.75
110	Yes	$6.75	Buy ABC at prevailing stock price, sell at $100	−$3.25
115	Yes	$6.75	Buy ABC at prevailing stock price, sell at $100	−$8.25
120	Yes	$6.75	Buy ABC at prevailing stock price, sell at $100	−$13.25
125	Yes	$6.75	Buy ABC at prevailing stock price, sell at $100	−$18.25

130	Yes	$6.75	Buy ABC at prevailing stock price, sell at $100	–$23.25

The spreadsheet for this exercise can be found at https://www.liverpooluniversitypress.co.uk/pages/essentials-of-financial-management-efm. Please ensure you click on Section 9 and the 9.4 tab at the bottom of the spreadsheet.

Net Profit vs. Terminal Stock Price for a Short Call

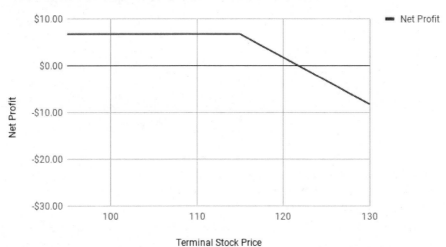

The payoff profile to the writer of a call option is the mirror image to that of the buyer of a call option. The maximum upside is limited to the premium received, whereas the downside is unlimited as potentially the underlying asset price could rise to infinity. This trade-off of limited reward versus unlimited risk may seem unattractive, but the cash received may be attractive to some investors with a particularly high-risk appetite.

9.5 Long put purchase

Suppose an investor buys a put option on ABC stock with an exercise price (X) of $100 at a put premium (P) of $3.79. In simple terms, this option gives the holder the right, but not the obligation, to sell ABC stock for $100. What we have to determine is what factors will lead to the option being exercised or thrown away.

Put premium = $3.79

Put strike = $100

Terminal stock price	Exercise?	Premium	Profit from exercising	Net profit
80	Yes	$3.79	$20.00	$16.21
85	Yes	$3.79	$15.00	$11.21
90	Yes	$3.79	$10.00	$6.21
95	Yes	$3.79	$5.00	$1.21
100	Yes/No	$3.79	$0.00	−$3.79
105	No	$3.79	$0.00	−$3.79
110	No	$3.79	$0.00	−$3.79
115	No	$3.79	$0.00	−$3.79
120	No	$3.79	$0.00	−$3.79
125	No	$3.79	$0.00	−$3.79
130	No	$3.79	$0.00	−$3.79

The spreadsheet for this exercise can be found at https://www.liverpooluniversitypress.co.uk/pages/essentials-of-financial-management-efm. Please ensure you click on Section 9 and the 9.5 tab at the bottom of the spreadsheet.

If the stock price is $120 on the expiration date will the investor exercise their put option? Of course not! Why would they sell the stock for $100 in the option market if they could sell it for $120 in the cash market? If the stock price is $110 on the expiration date will the investor exercise their put option? Again of course not. And so on for $109, $108 ... $101. Note that regardless of whether the option is exercised or not the investor must still pay the premium, $3.79.

However, if the stock price is $100 the investor is indifferent between selling the stock in the cash market and the options market. What about stock prices below $100? At stock prices below $100 such as $99 and $98 it is advantageous for the investor to sell the stock in the options contract rather than selling it in the cash market. But the investor paid $3.79 for the option, so they are effectively receiving $96.21 (i.e. $100 − $3.79) for the stock. So although it is advantageous for the investor to exercise their option, in reality it would have been better not to have purchased the option at all. If the stock price is below $96.21 on expiration, not only is it advantageous for the option to be exercised, it is in fact profitable. For example, if the stock price is $90 the investor could buy the stock in the cash market for $90, then sell the stock for $100 by the terms of the option contract. The profit, net of the premium, is then $7.21.

Following this logic, it is possible to map out a relationship between the stock price and profit/loss from exercising the option.

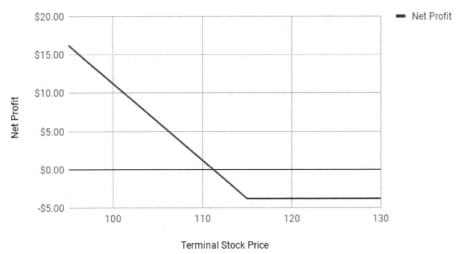

Net Profit vs. Terminal Stock Price for a Long Put

The profit facing the buyer of a put option is potentially large, though not unlimited, as the underlying asset price can never fall below zero. Like the call purchase, the maximum loss equals the premium paid. As a long put is profitable following a price decline, it is attractive to investors with a bearish view of the underlying asset.

9.6 Naked put write

The payoff profile to the writer of a put option is the mirror image to that of the buyer of a put option. A put option offers investors the right, but not the obligation, to sell a given asset at an agreed price on or before the expiry date. If the writer of such an option does not have a short position in the underlying asset, they are said to be naked. Hence, the fourth fundamental option strategy involves the sale of a put in which the seller does not have a short position in the underlying stock. Such a position is known as a naked put write. The profit and loss for a naked put write option position is detailed below:

Put premium = $3.79				
Put strike = $100				
Terminal stock price	Exercise?	Premium received	Action by writer	Net profit
80	Yes	$3.79	Buy stock at $100, sell at the market price	−$16.21
85	Yes	$3.79	Buy stock at $100, sell at the market price	−$11.21
90	Yes	$3.79	Buy stock at $100, sell at the market price	−$6.21
95	Yes	$3.79	Buy stock at $100, sell at the market price	−$1.21
100	Yes/No	$3.79	Nothing	$3.79
105	No	$3.79	Nothing	$3.79
110	No	$3.79	Nothing	$3.79
115	No	$3.79	Nothing	$3.79
120	No	$3.79	Nothing	$3.79
125	No	$3.79	Nothing	$3.79
130	No	$3.79	Nothing	$3.79

The profit profile for this strategy is shown below:

The spreadsheet for this exercise can be found at https://www.liverpooluniversitypress.co.uk/pages/essentials-of-financial-management-efm. Please ensure you click on Section 9 and the 9.6 tab at the bottom of the spreadsheet.

9.7 Long and short straddle strategies

In section 9.3 we introduced a long call strategy, whereby an investor with a bullish view of the market generates profit if the underlying asset price rises. In section 9.4 we introduced a long put strategy, where an investor with a bearish view of the market generates profit if the underlying asset price falls. What if an investor does not have a view on the direction of the market but is bullish on volatility? In this case, they could form a long call strategy and also a long put strategy with the same strike price and the same expiration date. This is referred to as a long straddle strategy.

Profit Profile for a long straddle

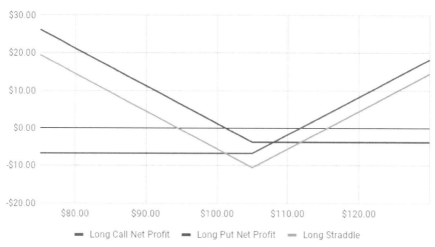

— Long Call Net Profit — Long Put Net Profit — Long Straddle

The V-shaped line in the diagram above is referred to as a long straddle. The worst possible outcome is if the price does not move, and the maximum loss occurs if the underlying asset price, at expiry, equals the strike price. The straddle has two break-even points, $89.46 and $110.54, i.e. the strike price of $100 minus the combined premiums of $10.54, and $100 plus the combined premiums.

The spreadsheet for this exercise can be found at https://www.liverpooluniversitypress.co.uk/pages/essentials-of-financial-management-efm. Please ensure you click on Section 9 and the 9.7 tab at the bottom of the spreadsheet.

An inverted V-shaped line can be created by selling a call and selling a put. An investor who forms such a strategy has a neutral view of market direction and a bearish view of future volatility. As this involves options being sold, the maximum profit is equal to the sum of the put and call premiums and is achieved when the underlying asset price, at expiry, equals the strike price. Sizeable, and potentially unlimited, losses occur if the underlying asset price moves significantly in either direction.

Profit Profile for a short straddle

9.8 The Black–Scholes option pricing model

Up until now the premiums have been given and we have not questioned how they are calculated. To best understand how premiums are determined it is important to consider the profit profiles for the buyer and writer of options. In particular, it is important to note that the buyer of the option has all of the "power" and will ultimately decide to exercise or not exercise the option. The maximum gain, however, for the writer is the premium. The writer therefore hopes that the option is not exercised. In valuing the option, factors that would mean the option is more likely to be exercised, such as high volatility or a longer time to maturity, will be reflected in a higher premium. The position of the underlying asset price relative to the strike price is another important factor.

The Black–Scholes[1] equation for valuing European call options, on non-dividend paying stocks, is:

$$C = SN(d_1) - Xe^{-rT}N(d_2)$$

---

[1] Named after the developers of the model, Fisher Black and Myron Scholes.

$$d_1 = \frac{\ln\left(\frac{S}{X}\right) + \left[r + \frac{1}{2}\sigma^2\right]T}{\sigma\sqrt{T}}$$

$$d_2 = d_1 - \sigma\sqrt{T}$$

where:

T = time to expiration (years)

N(.) = cumulative normal probability

C = fair value of the option

S = the current price of the stock

r = the risk-free rate of interest

X = exercise price of the option

σ = annualised standard deviation of the stock return

Consider the case of an ABC 50 call that expires in three months (T = .25) in which ABC stocks are trading at $45 and have an estimated annualised standard deviation of 0.5, and in which the risk-free rate is 6%. Plugging the values into the Black–Scholes formulae:

$$d_1 = \frac{\ln\left(\frac{45}{50}\right) + \left[0.06 + \frac{1}{2}0.5^2\right] \times 0.25}{0.5\sqrt{025}} = -0.2364$$

$$d_2 = -0.2364 - 0.5\sqrt{0.25} = -0.4864$$

From the normal distribution tables:

N(−0.2364) = 0.4065

N(−0.4864) = 0.3133

Putting all this together:

$$C = 45 \times 0.4065 - 50e^{-0.05\times.25} \times 0.3133 = \$2.86$$

The value of a corresponding put can be found using "put – call + parity":

$$P = C - S + Xe^{-rT} = \$2.86 - \$45 + 50e^{-0.06 \times .25} = \$7.12$$

The spreadsheet for this exercise can be found at https://www.liverpooluniversitypress.co.uk/pages/essentials-of-financial-management-efm. Please ensure you click on Section 9 and the 9.8 tab at the bottom of the spreadsheet.

Robert Merton extended the Black–Scholes model to incorporate the valuation of options on dividend paying stocks. In 1997 Robert Merton and Myron Scholes received the Nobel Prize in

Economic Sciences for developing a new method to determine the value of derivatives. Fisher Black died in 1995.

9.9 FX options as foreign currency insurance

In Chapter 7 we used forward contracts to hedge against movements in the exchange rate. The examples taught us that if the exchange rate moves in an unfavourable direction, then we will, in hindsight, be glad we hedged the risk. However, if the exchange rate moves in a favourable direction, then we will wish, in hindsight, that we had not hedged, since it would have been preferable to have waited and bought (or sold) the currency at the prevailing market price.

Foreign currency options exist that provide the right, but not the obligation, to buy (an FX call option) or to sell (an FX put option) foreign currency at a pre-agreed price.

An individual with foreign currency to sell can use put options to establish a floor price on the domestic value of the foreign currency. A put option on £1 with an exercise price of $1.40/GBP will ensure that, in the event of the value of the GBP falling below $1.40, £1 can be sold for $1.40 anyway.

If the put option costs $0.01/GBP, this floor price can be approximated as:

$1.40/GBP – $0.01/GBP = $1.39/GBP

or the strike price minus the premium.

Similarly, an individual who has to buy foreign currency at some point in the future can use call options to establish a ceiling price on the domestic currency amount that will have to be paid to purchase the foreign currency. A call option on £1 with an exercise price of $1.40/GBP will ensure that, in the event that the value rises above $1.40/GBP, £1 can be bought for $1.40 anyway.

If the call option costs $0.01/GBP, this ceiling price can be approximated as:

$1.40/GBP + $0.01/GBP = $1.41/GBP

or the strike price plus the premium.

Example

A US company wants to lock in a maximum dollar value of €300m (i.e it wants to sell €300m and receive as many dollars as possible), and this amount is to be sold between 1 January and 30 June. What kind of option should the company buy? A put option on euros.

Suppose the company buys from its bank a June put option with a strike price of US$1.34/EUR. The put is American, so that it can be used at any time prior to expiration. How do we determine the premium?

There is a foreign currency equivalent of the Black–Scholes model with one additional input, the foreign interest rate.

Assuming that the maturity date is 6 months away, the strike price is US$1.34/EUR, the spot rate is US$1.34/EUR, the volatility is 10 % p.a., the US interest rate is 0.5% p.a. and the euro interest rate is 0.5% p.a., then the put premium is US$0.0377/EUR or 3.77 cents per EUR.

The outcome is illustrated graphically below.

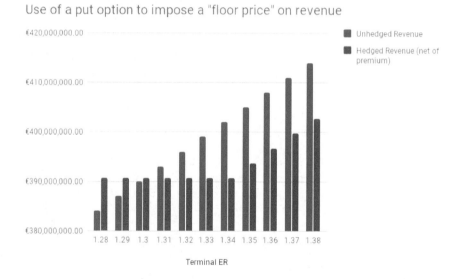

Use of a put option to impose a "floor price" on revenue

If the EUR depreciates (i.e. the spot rate drops below US$1.34/EUR), then the company will exercise its put option and receive US$402m:

$$€300m \times US\$1.34/EUR = \$402m$$

However, it must pay the premium of €300m x US$0.0377/EUR = US$11.31m, to give a net revenue of US$390.69m.

This is represented by the flat component of the red bars.

This can also be expressed as USD per EUR:

$$US\$390.69m/€300m = US\$1.3023/EUR$$

Note this can also be expressed as:

strike price – premium = US$1.34/EUR – US$0.0377/EUR = US$1.3023/EUR.

When the EUR appreciates (i.e. the spot rate is above US$1.34/EUR) the put option is not exercised and the €300m is sold in the spot market instead. Note that the premium is paid whether the option is exercised or not.

As we go from the left-hand side to the right-hand side, the EUR appreciates against the USD and the unhedged revenue (blue bars) increases.

The spreadsheet for this exercise can be found at https://www.liverpooluniversitypress.co.uk/ pages/essentials-of-financial-management-efm. Please ensure you click on Section 9 and the 9.9a tab at the bottom of the spreadsheet.

Example

A US importer will have a net cash outflow of £5m in payment for goods bought. The payment date is not known with certainty, but should occur in late June. The importer locks into a ceiling price for pounds by buying calls on the pound, with a strike price of US$1.56/GBP and an expiration date in June. If the current spot rate is US$1.56/GBP, what is the US importer worried about?

Since it has to make a payment of £5m which it must obtain by selling dollars, it is worried that in the meantime the value of the GBP will appreciate so that it costs more dollars to buy the £5m.

Assuming that the maturity date is 6 months away, the strike price is US$1.56/GBP, the spot rate is US$1.56/GBP, the volatility is 10% p.a., the US interest rate is 0.5% p.a. and the GBP interest rate is 2%p.a., then the premium for a European call is US$0.0382/GBP or 3.82 cents per GBP.

The outcome is illustrated graphically below.

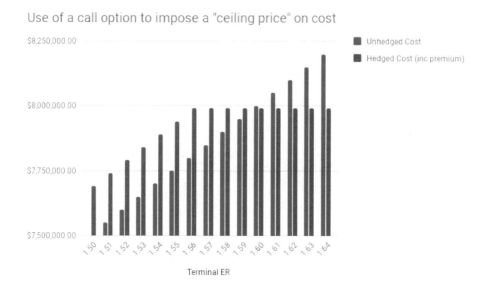

If the GBP appreciates (i.e. the spot rate goes above US$1.56/GBP), the company will exercise its option and pay US$7.8m. However, it must pay the premium of:

US$0.0382/GBP x £5m = US$0.19m

to give a net cost of US$7.99m, which is represented by the flat component of the red bars.

This can also be expressed as USD per GBP:

£5m/US$7.99m = US$1.5982/GBP

Note this can also be expressed as:

strike price + premium = US$1.56/GBP + US$0.0382/GBP = US$1.5982/GBP

As we go from the left-hand side to the right-hand side, the GBP appreciates against the USD. This is represented by the blue bars increasing in size. When the GBP depreciates, the call option is not exercised and the £5m is purchased in the spot market instead. Note that the premium is paid whether the option is exercised or not.

The spreadsheet for this exercise can be found at https://www.liverpooluniversitypress.co.uk/pages/essentials-of-financial-management-efm. Please ensure you click on Section 9 and the 9.9b tab at the bottom of the spreadsheet.

Activity 9.1

A US company faces a bill in three months' time of £750,000. In order to hedge the exchange rate risk the company buys a call option on £750,000 with a strike price of US$1.53/GBP and a premium of 3.03 cents per GBP. To reduce the cost of the hedge, the company simultaneously sells a put option on £750,000 with a strike price of US$1.49/GBP and a premium of 2.95 cents per GBP.

Evaluate this hedge at the following exchange rates from US$1.45 per GBP through to US$0.57 per GBP in increments of 1 cent.

Solution to activities

From Certificate of Incorporation of Alphabet[1]

This Corporation is authorized to issue nine billion (9,000,000,000) shares of Class A Common Stock, par value $0.001 per share (the "Class A Common Stock"), three billion (3,000,000,000) shares of Class B Common Stock, par value $0.001 per share (the "Class B Common Stock", and together with the Class A Common Stock, the "Common Stock"), three billion (3,000,000,000) shares of Class C Capital Stock, par value $0.001 per share (the "Class C Capital Stock"), and one hundred million (100,000,000) shares of Preferred Stock, par value $0.001 per share. The number of authorized shares of any class or classes of stock may be increased or decreased (but not below the number of shares thereof then outstanding) by the affirmative vote of the holders of at least a majority of the voting power of the issued and outstanding shares of Common Stock of the Corporation, voting together as a single class.

Except as otherwise provided herein or by applicable law, the holders of shares of Class A Common Stock and Class B Common Stock shall at all times vote together as one class on all matters (including the election of directors) submitted to a vote or for the consent of the stockholders of the Corporation. (ii) Each holder of shares of Class A Common Stock shall be entitled to one (1) vote for each share of Class A Common Stock held as of the applicable date

---

[1] https://www.sec.gov/Archives/edgar/data/1652044/000119312515336577/d82837dex31.htm

on any matter that is submitted to a vote or for the consent of the stockholders of the Corporation. (iii) Each holder of shares of Class B Common Stock shall be entitled to ten (10) votes for each share of Class B Common Stock held as of the applicable date on any matter that is submitted to a vote or for the consent of the stockholders of the Corporation.

Dividends. Subject to the preferences applicable to any series of Preferred Stock, if any, outstanding at any time, the holders of Class A Common Stock and the holders of Class B Common Stock shall be entitled to share equally, on a per share basis, in such dividends and other distributions of cash, property or shares of stock of the Corporation as may be declared by the Board of Directors from time to time with respect to the Common Stock out of assets or funds of the Corporation legally available therefor; provided, however, that in the event that such dividend is paid in the form of shares of Common Stock or rights to acquire Common Stock, the holders of Class A Common Stock shall receive Class A Common Stock or rights to acquire Class A Common Stock, as the case may be, and the holders of Class B Common Stock shall receive Class B Common Stock or rights to acquire Class B Common Stock, as the case may be.

The Alphabet 2016 annual report includes the following details:

> Our Class B common stock has 10 votes per share, our Class A common stock has one vote per share, and our Class C capital stock has no voting rights. As of December 31, 2016, Larry [Page], Sergey [Brin], and Eric [Schmidt] beneficially owned approximately 92.4% of our outstanding Class B common stock, which represented approximately 56.8% of the voting power of our outstanding capital stock.[2]

Therefore, while Alphabet's founders Larry Page and Sergey Brin (and founding CEO Eric Schmidt) may no longer have majority ownership of Alphabet's stock, they are able to maintain control due to the complex share structure of A, B and C shares.

---

[2] The 2016 annual report can be obtained from the Alphabet investor relations website available at https://abc.xyz/investor/pdf/2016_google_annual_report.pdf

Activity 1.2

> 23 June 2016 – 17,333.5
> 24 June 2016 – 16,088.10

Hence the FTSE250, which is predominantly made up of UK companies,[3] fell by 7% as a result of the referendum held on 23 June 2016 regarding the UK's membership of the EU. The drop in the index reflects what the market believes are the implications for the UK economy of leaving the EU, and the implications for these companies in particular. As an aside, many students may be asking why, in that case, the index has risen since? One possible explanation is that the exchange rate has fallen, which makes UK goods cheaper to overseas buyers. For example, on 23 June 2016 the USD/GBP exchange rate was US$1.4789/GBP, but by 3 January 2017 it had fallen to US$1.2282/GBP.

Activity 1.3

Up to October 2017, Microsoft has split its stock nine times, with six 2-for-1 splits and three 3-for-1 splits. After the most recent split, in 2003, one original share equals 288 shares. The current share price can be found at:

> https://uk.finance.yahoo.com/quote/MSFT/

As of 2 October 2017, the price was US$77.91. Multiplying this by 288, we obtain US$22,438.08, which represents a percentage return of 106,748% relative to the initial offer price of US$21 in March 1986.

Activity 2.1

Following the approach taken in section 2.1 we find the correlation to be –0.2873. This is not surprising given that crude oil is a major factor in the cost structure of an airline.

---

[3] http://www.londonstockexchange.com/exchange/prices-and-markets/stocks/indices/summary/summary-indices-constituents.html?index=MCX

The solution to this exercise can be found at https://www.liverpooluniversitypress.co.uk/pages/essentials-of-financial-management-efm. Please ensure you click on Activity Solutions and the Activity 2.1 tab at the bottom of the spreadsheet.

Activity 2.2

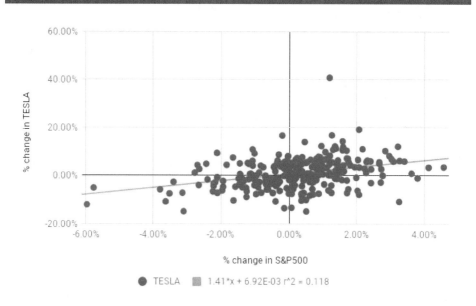

The beta of Tesla is 1.41, but the interesting point is that the r-squared is only 11.8%, indicating that Tesla is exposed to significantly more unique risks than market risks.

The solution to this exercise can be found at https://www.liverpooluniversitypress.co.uk/pages/essentials-of-financial-management-efm. Please ensure you click on Activity Solutions and the Activity 2.2 tab at the bottom of the spreadsheet.

Activity 2.3

Value of portfolio = 10,000 x 12.15 + 10,000 x 49.53 + 10,000 x 88.55 = 121,000 + 495,300 + 885,500 = 1,501,800

Weight in each:

121,000/1,501,800 = 8.06%, 495,300/1,501,800= 32.98%, 885,500/1,501,800= 58.96%

Beta of portfolio = .0806 x 1.13 + .3298 x 0.71 + .5896 x 0.52 = 0.65

A common mistake in this exercise is to use the weights of 1/3, 1/3 and 1/3, as the portfolio includes 10,000 of each stock. However, this does not reflect the fact that the stock's prices are all different and hence the wealth invested in each asset differs.

The solution to this exercise can be found at https://www.liverpooluniversitypress.co.uk/pages/essentials-of-financial-management-efm. Please ensure you click on Activity Solutions and the Activity 2.3 tab at the bottom of the spreadsheet.

Activity 3.1

At the time of writing (October 2017):

Highest: 31 March 2017 – 168.50, r= 8/168.50 = 4.7%

Lowest: 30 June 2016 – 138.875, r = 8/138.75 = 5.8%

The solution to this exercise can be found at https://www.liverpooluniversitypress.co.uk/pages/essentials-of-financial-management-efm. Please ensure you click on Activity Solutions and the Activity 3.1 tab at the bottom of the spreadsheet.

Activity 3.2

Alphabet

"We have never declared or paid any cash dividend on our common or capital stock. We intend to retain any future earnings and do not expect to pay any cash dividends in the foreseeable future."
(Alphabet Annual report, 2016, page 17)

Amazon

"We have never declared or paid cash dividends on our common stock."
(Amazon Annual report, 2016, page 16)

Imperial Brands

"The Board is pleased to be recommending a total dividend for the year of 155.2 pence per share, another strong increase of 10 per cent. This is the

eighth consecutive year that we have delivered dividend growth of 10 per cent and we are committed to maintaining this annual growth rate over the medium term."
(Imperial Tobacco Annual report, 2016, page 2)

Imperial Brands dividend history is also detailed at
http://www.imperialbrandsplc.com/Investors/Shareholder-centre/Dividends-history.html.

Activity 4.1

Par	€1,000	
Coupon	5.00%	<<You can edit this cell. The default is 5%
YTM	10.00%	<<You can edit this cell. The default is 10%

Year	CF	PV	t x PV	
1	€50.00	€45.45	€45.45	
2	€50.00	€41.32	€82.64	
3	€1,050	€788.88	€2,366.64	
	Price	€875.66	2,494.74	<< = sum of t x PV
	D	2.85		

$$D = \frac{1 \times \left(\frac{€50}{1.1}\right) + 2 \times \left(\frac{€50}{1.1^2}\right) + 3 \times \left(\frac{€1050}{1.1^3}\right)}{\left(\frac{€50}{1.1}\right) + \left(\frac{€50}{1.1^2}\right) + \left(\frac{€1050}{1.1^3}\right)}$$

$$= \frac{1 \times 45.45 + 2 \times 41.32 + 3 \times 788.88}{45.45 + 41.32 + 788.88}$$

$$\frac{2,494.73}{875.65} = 2.85$$

Activity 5.1

Year	0	1	2	3
Cash flow	−$60,000	$25,000	$25,000	$25,000
Cumulative cash flow	−$60,000	−$35,000	−$10,000	$15,000
Payback	2.4 years			

After two years this project still needs to return a further $10,000. As $25,000 of cash flows accrue in year 3, the payback is then $2 + \left|\frac{-10,000}{25,000}\right| = 2.4\ years.$

r	5.00%			
Year	0	1	2	3
Cash flow	−$60,000	$25,000	$25,000	$25,000
PV of cash flow	−$60,000	$23,809.52	$22,675.74	$21,595.94
Cumulative PV	−$60,000	−$36,190.48	−$13,514.74	$8,081.20
Modified payback	2.54 years			

After two years the project still needs to return a further $13,514.74. As $21,595.94 of present value of cash flows accrue in year 3, the payback is then $2 + \left|\frac{-13,514.74}{21,595.94}\right| = 2.54\ years.$

For any positive discount rate the present value of a cash flow is less than the actual level of the cash flow, hence it follows that modified payback is greater than simple payback.

The solution to this exercise can be found at https://www.liverpooluniversitypress.co.uk/pages/essentials-of-financial-management-efm. Please ensure you click on Activity Solutions and the Activity 5.1 tab at the bottom of the spreadsheet.

Activity 6.1

Beta	2
Rf	2%
E(Rm) – Rf	4%
Cost of equity = E(Ri)	10%

Price	610
Par	1000
T	5
Coupon	0

Price = Par/(1 + YTM)^5	
Cost of debt = YTM = ((par/price)$^{1/5}$) – 1=	10.39%
Tax rate	23%
Cost of debt after tax	8%

$$K_{WACC} = \left[K_E + K_{DAT} \times \frac{D}{E}\right] / \left[1 + \frac{D}{E}\right] = \left[0.1 + 0.08 \times \frac{1}{1}\right] / \left[1 + \frac{1}{1}\right] = 0.09 = 9\%$$

The solution to this exercise can be found at https://www.liverpooluniversitypress.co.uk/pages/essentials-of-financial-management-efm. Please ensure you click on Activity Solutions and the Activity 6.1 tab at the bottom of the spreadsheet.

Activity 7.1

$$F_{12/12}(DKK/EUR) = \frac{S(DKK/EUR) \times (1 + i_{DKK})}{(1 + i_{EUR})} = \frac{7.4422 \times (1 + 0.015)}{(1 + .0122)}$$
$$= 7.401 \, DKK/EUR$$

The solution to this exercise can be found at https://www.liverpooluniversitypress.co.uk/pages/essentials-of-financial-management-efm. Please ensure you click on Activity Solutions and the Activity 7.1 tab at the bottom of the spreadsheet.

Activity 8.1

Exposure = 200,000 bushels	
FV = 5,000	

Number of contracts	40

Initial basis	−10
Final basis	0
Go long at	872 cents per bushel
Spot	862 cents per bushel
Expected cost	$1,724,000

Spot Price	Futures Price	P/L on Futures	Cost of Wheat at Spot	Change in Cost	Net Cost	HE
820	820	$ -104,000.00	$ 1,640,000.00	$ -84,000.00	$ 1,744,000.00	123.8%
840	840	$ -64,000.00	$ 1,680,000.00	$ -44,000.00	$ 1,744,000.00	145.5%
860	860	$ -24,000.00	$ 1,720,000.00	$ -4,000.00	$ 1,744,000.00	600.0%
880	880	$ 16,000.00	$ 1,760,000.00	$ 36,000.00	$ 1,744,000.00	44.4%
900	900	$ 56,000.00	$ 1,800,000.00	$ 76,000.00	$ 1,744,000.00	73.7%
920	920	$ 96,000.00	$ 1,840,000.00	$ 116,000.00	$ 1,744,000.00	82.8%
940	940	$ 136,000.00	$ 1,880,000.00	$ 156,000.00	$ 1,744,000.00	87.2%

When the price of wheat rises, and the spot and futures prices converge, then the spot rate rises by a larger proportion than the futures prices. Hence the change in cost is larger than the profit on the futures position, and the hedge efficiency is less than 100%. However, when the prices fall (and converge), the spot price falls less than the futures price, and the hedge efficiency is greater than 100%.

If the basis remains constant at −10, the hedge efficiency is 100% as the spot and futures prices have moved in tandem.

Spot Price	Futures Price	P/L on Futures	Cost of Wheat at Spot	Change in Cost	Net Cost	HE
820	830	$ -84,000.00	$ 1,640,000.00	$ -84,000.00	$ 1,724,000.00	100.0%
840	850	$ -44,000.00	$ 1,680,000.00	$ -44,000.00	$ 1,724,000.00	100.0%
860	870	$ -4,000.00	$ 1,720,000.00	$ -4,000.00	$ 1,724,000.00	100.0%
880	890	$ 36,000.00	$ 1,760,000.00	$ 36,000.00	$ 1,724,000.00	100.0%
900	910	$ 76,000.00	$ 1,800,000.00	$ 76,000.00	$ 1,724,000.00	100.0%
920	930	$ 116,000.00	$ 1,840,000.00	$ 116,000.00	$ 1,724,000.00	100.0%
940	950	$ 156,000.00	$ 1,880,000.00	$ 156,000.00	$ 1,724,000.00	100.0%

The solution to this exercise can be found at https://www.liverpooluniversitypress.co.uk/pages/essentials-of-financial-management-efm. Please ensure you click on Activity Solutions and the Activity 8.1 tab at the bottom of the spreadsheet.

Activity 9.1

Expsoure=	£	750,000.00					
Call Strike=		1.53	USD/GBP	Call Premium=		3.03	cents per GBP
Put Strike		1.49	USD/GBP	Put premium=		2.95	cents per GBP
				Total premium=	$	600.00	

Spot Rate	Call Exercised?	Put Exercised	Buy pounds via	Cost	Cost after premium
1.350	No	Yes	Via Put	$ 1,117,500.00	$ 1,118,100.00
1.400	No	Yes	Via Put	$ 1,117,500.00	$ 1,118,100.00
1.450	No	Yes	Via Put	$ 1,117,500.00	$ 1,118,100.00
1.500	No	No	Via Spot	$ 1,125,000.00	$ 1,125,600.00
1.550	Yes	No	Via Call	$ 1,147,500.00	$ 1,148,100.00
1.600	Yes	No	Via Call	$ 1,147,500.00	$ 1,148,100.00
1.650	Yes	No	Via Call	$ 1,147,500.00	$ 1,148,100.00

Here to reduce the cost of the hedge, the company sells a put option with a lower strike price than the call option. If the holder exercises, they will be forced to buy (reluctantly) at US$1.40/GBP, though they would rather buy more cheaply in the spot market. The net effect is that the company creates a maximum cost and a minimum cost.

The solution to this exercise can be found at https://www.liverpooluniversitypress.co.uk/pages/essentials-of-financial-management-efm. Please ensure you click on Activity Solutions.

Bibliography

Articles

Graham, John R., and Harvey, Campbell R. 'The theory and practice of corporate finance: evidence from the field', *Journal of Financial Economics*, 60.2–3 (2001), pp. 187–243, https://doi.org/10.1016/S0304-405X(01)00044-7.

Miller, Merton H., and Modigliani, Franco, 'Dividend policy, growth, and the valuation of shares', *The Journal of Business*, 34.4 (1961), pp. 411–433.

Roll, Richard, 'A critique of the asset pricing theory's tests Part I: On past and potential testability of the theory', *Journal of Financial Economics*, 4.2 (1977), pp. 129–176.

Roll, Richard, and Ross, Stephen A. 'An empirical investigation of the Arbitrage Pricing Theory', *The Journal of Finance*, 35 (1980), pp. 1073–1103.

Sharpe, William F. 'Capital asset prices: a theory of market equilibrium under conditions of risk', *The Journal of Finance*, 19.3, (1964), pp. 425–442, https://doi.org/10.2307/2977928.

Books

Arnold, G. (2014). *Corporate Financial Management*. Harlow, United Kingdom: Pearson Education Limited.

Gordon, Myron J. (1962). *The Investment, Financing, and Valuation of the Corporation*. Homewood, Ill: R.D. Irwin.

Hull, J. (2017). *Fundamentals of futures and options markets*. Boston: Pearson.

Johnson, R., and Giacotto, C. (1995). *Options and Futures*. New York: West Publishing.

Luenberger, D. (2014). *Investment science*. New York: Oxford University Press.

Macaulay, Frederick (1938). *Some Theoretical Problems suggested by the Movements of Interest Rates, Bond Yields, and Stock Prices in the United States since 1856*. New York: Columbia University Press for the National Bureau of Economic Research.

Websites

2016 Google Annual Report, https://abc.xyz/investor/pdf/2016_google_annual_report.pdf

'Amended and Restated Certificate of Incorporation of Alphabet Inc.', https://www.sec.gov/Archives/edgar/data/1652044/000119312515336577/d82837dex31.htm

Apple, 'Investor Relations: Dividend History', http://investor.apple.com/dividends.cfm

Bank of China, 'Preference Shares', http://www.boc.cn/en/investor/ir4/201501/t20150114_4462474.html

Bank for International Settlements, Triennial Central Bank Survey: Foreign exchange turnover in April 2016, http://www.bis.org/publ/rpfx16fx.pdf

BP, 'Preference share dividends', https://www.bp.com/en/global/corporate/investors/information-forshareholders/dividends/preference-share-dividends.html

Citigroup, 'Stock Split History', http://www.citigroup.com/citi/investor/ajax/split.html

Credit Suisse, 'Credit Suisse Global Investment Returns Yearbook', Elroy Dimson, Paul Marsh, Mike Staunton, February 2017, https://publications.credit-suisse.com/tasks/render/file/?fileID=B8FDD84D-A4CD-D983-12840F52F61BA0B4

Imperial Brands, 'Dividend History', http://www.imperialbrandsplc.com/Investors/Shareholder-centre/Dividends-history.html

International Monetary Fund, 2016 Annual Report on Exchange Arrangements and Exchange Restrictions International Monetary Fund, https://www.imf.org/en/Publications/Annual-Report-on-Exchange-Arrangements-and-Exchange-Restrictions/Issues/2017/01/25/Annual-Report-on-Exchange-Arrangements-and-Exchange-Restrictions-2016-43741

London Stock Exchange, http://www.londonstockexchange.com/

London Stock Exchange, 'FTSE 250', http://www.londonstockexchange.com/exchange/prices-andmarkets/stocks/indices/summary/summary-indices-constituents.html?index=MCX

Nobelprize.org, 'Eugene F. Fama – Facts', Nobel Media 2014, https://www.nobelprize.org/nobel_prizes/economic-sciences/laureates/2013/fama-facts.html

Nobelprize.org, 'The Prize in Economics 1990 – Press Release', Nobel Media AB 2014, https://www.nobelprize.org/nobel_prizes/economic-sciences/laureates/1990/press.html

Speedy Hire Plc, Annual Report and Accounts 2017, https://www.speedyservices.com/uploads/file/3b3c1008195f47fdacf351108f221a1d/6899_Speedy_AR_2017_Web.pdf

Yahoo! Finance, Kellogg Company (K), https://uk.finance.yahoo.com/quote/K?p=K

Yahoo! Finance, Microsoft Corporation (MSFT), https://uk.finance.yahoo.com/quote/MSFT/

Yahoo! Finance, Walmart Inc. (WMT), https://uk.finance.yahoo.com/quote/WMT/?p=WMT

Yahoo! Finance, The Walt Disney Company (DIS), https://uk.finance.yahoo.com/quote/DIS/?p=DIS

Yahoo! Finance, Wynn Resorts, Limited (WEYNN), https://uk.finance.yahoo.com/quote/WYNN/?p=WYNN